Series/Number 07-125

D0862982

RELATING STATISTICS AND EXPERIMENTAL DESIGN
An Introduction

IRWIN P. LEVIN
University of Iowa

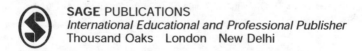

SAGE PUBLICATIONS
International Educational and Professional Publisher
Thousand Oaks   London   New Delhi

For information:

SAGE Publications, Inc.
2455 Teller Road
Thousand Oaks, California 91320
E-mail: order@sagepub.com

SAGE Publications Ltd.
6 Bonhill Street
London EC2A 4PU
United Kingdom

SAGE Publications India Pvt. Ltd.
M-32 Market
Greater Kailash I
New Delhi 110 048 India

Printed in the United States of America

Library of Congress Cataloging-in-Publication Data

Levin, Irwin P.
    Relating statistics and experimental design: an introduction / by Irwin P. Levin.
      p. cm. — (Quantitative applications in the social sciences ; v. 125)
    Includes bibliographical references.
    ISBN 0-7619-1472-2
1. Experimental design. 2. Analysis of variance. I. Title. II. Series: Sage university papers series. Quantitative applications in the social sciences ; no. 07-125.
  QA179.L48 1999
  001.4′34—dc21   98-40176

02 03 04 10 9 8 7 6 5 4 3

Acquiring Editor:	C. Deborah Laughton
Editorial Assistant:	Eileen Carr
Production Editor:	Astrid Virding
Production Assistant:	Denise Santoyo
Typesetter:	Technical Typesetting Inc.

When citing a university paper, please use the proper form. Remember to cite the Sage University Paper series title and include the paper number. One of the following formats can be adapted (depending on the style manual used):

(1) LEVIN, I. P. (1998) *Relating Statistics and Experimental Design: An Introduction.* Sage University Papers Series on Quantitative Applications in the Social Sciences, 07-125. Thousand Oaks, CA: Sage.

OR

(2) Levin, I. P. (1998). *Relating statistics and experimental design: An Introduction* (Sage University Papers Series on Quantitative Applications in the Social Sciences, series no. 07-125). Thousand Oaks, CA: Sage.

CONTENTS

SERIES EDITOR'S INTRODUCTION

Good research comes from practice. Novice graduate students begin to apply their learning in the lab and improve through repetition and instruction. Eventually they "get it right," if all goes well, but the process is frustrating. It is frustrating because they tend to feel behind in their knowledge of design and analysis, which they are still learning, usually in a course sequence that spreads over some semesters. The problem is it is necessary to have all the research tools at the ready, the sooner the better. Hence, the value of methods texts that give the big picture, view and review, and integrate, like the monograph at hand.

Dr. Levin gives the budding researcher, say an honors senior in the social sciences or a first-year graduate student in psychology, a clear description of the standard tools of the trade. The fundamentals of design are covered and, although the focus is on experiments, observational methods also receive attention. Then there is an exposition of major tests of significance, with formulas plus easy verbal interpretations. Finally, in a contribution that is unique, research designs are matched to their proper statistical tests. This integration is invaluable because it is often the case that the two—design and statistics—are taught independently, leaving the student to figure out what goes with what. One pedagogical device is "boxes" embedded in the text that contain prototypic applications. There are ten of these boxes that give applications of the following tests: a t test for two independent random groups design, a t test for repeated measures design, a median test to two independent random groups design, a Mann–Whitney U test for comparing two independent groups, a one-way ANOVA to independent random groups design with more than two levels, a two-way ANOVA to factorial design, a chi-square for a single categorical variable, a chi-square for a test of contingency between two categorical variables, a correlation coefficient for an observed relationship between two variables, and a multiple regression equation.

Once students internalize the applications given in the boxes, they can draw on the examples to understand a wide range of comparable research situations. For instance, Box 4.1 illustrates the application of a t test for a two independent random groups design. The general research question is whether watching television violence encourages aggressive behavior among children. Fifty 8-year-old boys are randomly assigned to two groups: one exposed to violent TV programming; the other exposed to nonviolent TV programming. Afterward, they are observed to see how aggressive they are at play. The t ratio of 2.97 exceeds the critical value, so the null hypothesis is rejected in favor of the alternative hypothesis, that watching TV violence increased the number of acts of aggression. The student, upon recalling this illustration, will have in mind the design and analysis basics when the research issue is whether a simple change in an independent variable X (treatment vs. no treatment) has an effect on some behavior Y.

Professor Levin offers valuable general guidelines for relating statistics to design. He makes the particularly important point that the choice of statistical test depends heavily on how the dependent variable is measured. Continuous (interval or ratio) response variables suggest a t test when X has two levels or an F test in a one-way ANOVA when X has more than two levels. Noncontinuous response variables may suggest a chi-square test if data are nominal or a Mann–Whitney test if data are ordinal. While sensitizing the student to the choice of statistics, he offers the sage reminder that "Even the most sophisticated statistical test will not rescue a poorly designed study." This monograph will lead the beginning research worker to better combine research design and statistical analysis. It is an ideal first reading assignment in research methods for the incoming graduate student in the experimental social sciences.

—*Michael S. Lewis-Beck*
Series Editor

ACKNOWLEDGMENTS

The author gratefully acknowledges helpful suggestions from two valued University of Iowa colleagues, Bob Forsyth of the College of Education and Bob Kirby of the Department of Psychology, and some wonderful students, Jenny Larkins, Kirsten Redalen, and Dean Yoshizumi. Thanks also to Mike Lewis-Beck for his support and encouragement, and to two anonymous reviewers who contributed greatly to the shaping of this monograph.

RELATING STATISTICS AND EXPERIMENTAL DESIGN
An Introduction

IRWIN P. LEVIN
University of Iowa

1. INTRODUCTION AND OVERVIEW

A group of students in a laboratory course I recently taught on behavioral research conducted a study of college drinking behavior. They were particularly interested in the role of fraternal organizations in promoting such behavior. Among the questions they investigated were: (1) Do members of "Greek" organizations (fraternities and sororities) drink more than non Greeks? (2) Is this true for both males and females? (3) Were students who joined Greek organizations more apt to have been drinkers in high school and to what extent does this account for their current drinking behavior? To answer these questions, the students collected data from Greeks and non-Greeks that included estimates of frequency and amount of drinking both before and after starting college.

With the multiple questions they were asking, what statistical tests should the researchers have performed to extract the most out of their data? Why those particular tests? What is the logic behind their use? What will the tests of significance tell them beyond the calculation of descriptive measures such as averages? What are the limitations of these tests?

The task was particularly difficult for the students because, although they were very much interested in what their data had to tell them, they were not fully prepared to perform the appropriate data analyses. They had taken an elementary statistics course that taught them how to use the standard tests, but they had never faced the task of *selecting* the most appropriate test in an actual research setting. The average introductory statistics class and the textbook that accompanies it provide separate sections on each major statistical test, usually presented in a standard order such as z test, t test, χ^2, correlation and regression, and analysis of variance. There are exer-

1

cises at the end of each chapter and tests at the end of each section that provide examples of the use of that particular statistic. This format often leads students simply to use the test that they recently have been studying, rather than actually thinking about which test is appropriate.

This, of course, is not the way things are in actual research settings. Researchers face the task of selecting the appropriate test(s) based on the way the study was designed and executed (e.g., what measures of behavior were taken). This monograph emphasizes the problem-solving task of deciding which statistical test to use in which research setting. Indeed, the researcher who does not see the inherent connection between experimental design and statistics may end up with a set of data that defy direct tests of the hypotheses of interest. Fortunately, the connection, once one sees it, is often straightforward and logical. For example, measuring a potentially important subject characteristic such as gender not only makes logical sense in designing an experiment, but its incorporation into the statistical plan for analyzing the data adds greatly to the interpretation of the results. This monograph emphasizes the logical development of rules for determining the appropriate test to use in a variety of common research settings.

This monograph is organized as follows: We start with a section describing common behavioral research approaches and methods, with an initial emphasis on the logic behind the choice of each approach and method, distinguishing between *causal relationships* uncovered with the experimental method and relationships uncovered with other methods that do not imply cause and effect. Later in this section, we describe specific experimental designs that illustrate a variety of ways to achieve experimental control. The next section concerns standard statistical tests. Before describing the most common specific tests, we develop the general logic behind the use of testing statistical significance. We identify the development of statistical hypothesis testing as a major breakthrough in the history of science, yet recommend caution in interpreting statistical results. In describing specific statistical tests, we emphasize their boundary conditions and domains of application, and leave it to other sources for mathematical and computational development. Technical terms printed in Italics and that deal with statistical and design concepts are defined briefly in the text and more completely in a glossary at the end of the monograph.

One thing to note from the beginning is the different language employed by statisticians in describing the use of their tests and working social scientists in applying these tests to the data obtained from a research study. The statistician talks about the likelihood of obtaining a certain statistical result contingent upon a particular set of mathematical assumptions. The researcher, on the other hand, talks about whether the factors of interest in the study did or did not have their predicted effect. Learning about social science research requires both an understanding of research design and a knowledge of basic statistical concepts.

The cornerstone of this monograph is the section linking research design and statistics. Developing this linkage requires both an understanding of the complementary roles of research design and statistics, and learning to select the appropriate statistical test for a particular research design. One way to learn which statistical test goes with which type of study is to think of prototypical examples. Examples are chosen from research topics that should be of general interest, such as assessing the effectiveness of clinical therapies, examining gender differences in voting preferences, demonstrating drug interaction effects, examining the relationship between violence on television and aggressive behavior in children, and predicting performance in college. Each example addresses both research design and statistical concerns by including operational definitions of the variables of interest in the study; selection of the appropriate statistical test; specification of the relevant statistical hypotheses; a scheme for how the data are to be collected, organized, and compiled; application of statistical formulas; and appropriate decisions and conclusions based on both the design of the study and the statistical results. This section ends with a rather extensive table that summarizes these examples and a flow diagram to be used as an aid for selecting the most appropriate statistical test. Finally, we return to see what our intrepid students found in studying college drinking behavior.

2. BASIC EXPERIMENTAL DESIGNS

In this section we describe the most commonly used research designs and discuss the major issues that govern the choice of design.

2.1. General Considerations

A general issue to be addressed in various parts of this monograph is *causality*. How can statistical relationships be used to establish that changes in one variable are responsible for causing changes in another variable? Are particular research designs more effective in determining causality than others? In the sciences there are different levels of explanation. For example, the political scientist may explain why a particular election result turned out as it did by analyzing the degree of agreement or disagreement among the populace with the various stances taken by the candidates. The experimental psychologist may explain why food-deprived rats run faster down the alley than nondeprived rats by appealing to differences in motivation. The brain scientist may not be satisfied with any explanation of learning or memory that cannot be tied to neural mechanisms in the brain. In each of these cases, the key is to show that changes in one or a small number of factors preceded changes in the target behavior and that other factors either did not change (i.e., were held constant) while the behavior was shown to change or that changes in these other factors were inconsequential. In particular, we show that the experimental method, by manipulating and controlling potential causal variables, is the best method for identifying specific factors as the causes of a particular behavior.[1]

Social scientists often strive to identify specific factors as the causes of the behavior they are investigating. This requires systematic manipulation of the factors they are focusing on, while holding all other factors constant. The most direct way to accomplish this is the *experimental method*. At other times, researchers may be particularly concerned that control achieved through the use of artificial and idiosyncratic sets of experimental conditions may limit the ability to generalize their findings to real-life situations. An alternative course of action is to carefully and systematically observe behavior and its antecedents in the absence of outside intervention. This is the *method of observation*. Both of these approaches, the experimental method and the method of observation, if applied carefully, can yield valuable insights. Researchers using either method must be aware of potential sources of bias in their studies and seek to eliminate them.

2.2. Basic Research Methods

2.2.1. The Experimental Method

This is the method of choice when the researcher is primarily interested in determining cause and effect. The experimental method is characterized by the manipulation of one or more variables called *independent variables* and the control of all others. *Manipulation* means creating or selecting discrete levels of a variable and comparing responses across levels. *Control* means holding an *extraneous variable* (a variable other than an independent variable that may influence the results of an experiment) constant across levels of the independent variable. If the researcher is successful in achieving control over all extraneous variables, then he or she can determine that changes in behavior (the *dependent variable* or variables) must have been caused by the manipulation of the independent variable.

Consider the following example. A psychologist claims to have developed a "smart pill" that improves human memory. A good way to test this claim is to use *randomization*, for example, to assign subjects at random to two different conditions: a condition where subjects receive the pill before being given the memory task and a condition where subjects do not receive the pill. Although more sophisticated methods will be described later, one simple way to assign subjects at random to conditions is to flip a coin for each successive pair of subjects. If the coin comes up heads, the first subject receives the drug and the second subject does not. If the coin comes up tails, the opposite assignment is used. This method assures that each subject has a 50:50 chance of being assigned to either condition. The researcher has thereby *manipulated* a variable: whether or not the subject receives the pill. This variable is called the *independent variable*, and the two conditions represent the two levels of the independent variable. To determine the effect of the pill, the researcher compares performance on the memory task between the two groups. The measure of performance, such as the number of errors made on the task, is called the *dependent variable*. There are a number of other variables, called *extraneous variables* because they are not the focus of the study, that could affect performance on the task. These include *subject characteristics*, such as intelligence or motivation, and *task characteristics*, such as the material to be memorized and how, when, and where it is presented. The goal of the researcher who is attempting to isolate the effect of the independent variable on the dependent variable is to *control* these extraneous factors, which means to equate them across levels of the independent variable. Random assignment of subjects to conditions is one way to control subject characteristics. Task characteristics are controlled by paying careful attention to the details of conducting the experiment: use exactly the same material, presented at the same pace, to subjects in each condition. Use the same room and perhaps even the same time of day (which could potentially influence memory) for both conditions. Variations of these ways to achieve control are illustrated in the specific experimental design techniques to be described shortly.

Statistical inferences are based on the notion that research data represent a random sample from some identifiable population where each member of the population has an equal chance of being selected for the sample. However, the statistician's concept of *random sampling* often gets compromised in the application of the experimental method in social sciences research. If a study is to employ college students, random sampling would require using a computer to generate random samples from a listing of student ID numbers and the students with those number would constitute the subjects of the study. In practice, "handy samples" are used, such as a classroom of students or "volunteers" who sign up to meet a class requirement or to earn extra money. The "population" represented by such samples is difficult to define. The social scientist is apt to argue that the processes or behavioral principles tapped in the study are, themselves, generalizable beyond the samples used in the study. With the limited ability to generate random samples, social scientists can, nevertheless, take their handy sample and, within it, assign subjects at random to different experimental conditions so that there is no bias due, for example, to assigning initial volunteers to one condition and later volunteers to another.

Among the subtle influences on behavior that must be controlled through good experimental techniques are subject biases and experimenter biases. *Subject biases* may arise when subjects' beliefs about what they should do in an experiment affect their responses. An experiment whose goals are transparent may produce biased respond-ing. For example, subjects who know that their attitudes toward different racial groups are being assessed may project a more positive image than they would ordinarily display. *Experimenter bias* can occur when the experimenter's measurement and treatment of the data influence the outcome of research. This is most likely to occur when the experimenter has strong expectancies about how the data should turn out and when elements of subjectivity enter into scoring and recording data. For example, a researcher may be particularly in-vested in demonstrating the utility of a new drug. To counter such biasing effects, a "double-blind" technique can be used where nei-ther the subject in a drug study nor the experimenter knows whether the subject is in the drug or placebo condition. A third person (or a computer) keeps track of which subject is in which condition. Mecha-nized techniques for recording responses can also combat biases.

Control over potentially biasing influences is most readily achieved in a well-defined laboratory setting. However, if conditions of the laboratory setting are very different from conditions that exist in the real world, then results of laboratory research may be questioned due to their limited applicability outside the laboratory setting. For exam-ple, the number and magnitude of errors in judgment may be different in a driving simulator than in actual driving situations. Nevertheless, factors like fatigue and alcohol use may have similar effects in both situations, yet can be studied more safely in the simulator.

2.2.2. The Method of Observation

This method relies on careful observation, recording, and classifi-cation of behavior to determine relationships between variables. The method of observation is most often used when manipulation of the behavior of interest is not possible for practical or ethical reasons. For example, naturalistic observation may permit investigation of factors such as stress over much wider ranges than would be feasible in the laboratory. Observation would then focus systematically on situational factors preceding heightened levels of stress and/or indi-vidual's reactions to the stress. As pointed out by Levin and Hinrichs (1995), careful selection of behaviors and conditions for the purpose of relating them to each other through the method of observation can serve many of the same purposes as selecting independent and dependent variables using the experimental method.

Observation of behavior in natural settings does not carry with it the concern for reality that there was with the experimental method. Despite the reality of the setting, however, many precautions must be taken to preserve the validity of an observational study. In particular, the observer must avoid intruding on the behavior being observed and must avoid being influenced by prior expectancies and hypotheses. Just as there are potential subject biases in using the experimental method, participants in an observational study might behave differently if they know they are being observed. Consequently, the researcher must observe from afar or must take the time needed for the subjects of the observation to get used to the presence of the observer. Jane Goodall's long-term observation of chimpanzees in the wild is an example.

Another major concern with the method of observation is the representativeness of the behavior being recorded. The behavior of people in a crowded setting may be quite different if the crowds are assembled purposely, such as attendance at an athletic event or a concert, than if crowding is involuntary, such as during rush hour traffic. The key here is to describe the antecedent conditions as well as the observed behavior, and to resist generalizing from one set of conditions to another. In this regard, the concerns are similar for research using the observational method and the experimental method.

The major problem facing users of the method of observation is that it is more difficult to identify cause and effect. Many factors may vary together in an uncontrolled setting, and it is difficult, if not impossible, to separate their effects. An observed relationship between variables A and B could be due to the influence of A on B, the influence of B on A, or it could be that a third variable C influences both A and B. For example, suppose that a positive correlation was reported between the number of Automatic Teller Machines (ATMs) and the crime rate in different parts of a large city. It could mean that the presence of ATMs attracted criminals who prey on people withdrawing money at night, or it could mean that people who live in areas of high crime rate are less apt to carry large sums of money and thus have more need for frequent trips to the ATM, or it could mean merely that areas of higher population density have both higher crime rate and more ATMs. Sometimes it is possible to at least partially disentangle such a confusing web of causality through the use of *longitudinal studies*, studies that track successive changes in events over time. Does the crime rate increase immediately after opening new ATMs or vice versa? Data of this kind can help sort out cause and effect, even though no experimental manipulation was involved. Sciences such as astronomy advance through careful and systematic observation over long periods of time.

Some studies combine elements of both the experimental and observational methods to achieve control over some variables while allowing others to vary naturally.[2] Such studies are sometimes called *quasi-experimental* because, like an experiment, they attempt to isolate the effect of one factor by controlling as many other factors as possible. However, they lack the element of random assignment, which eliminates bias in the assignment of subjects to experimental conditions by assuring that each subject has the same chance of being assigned to any given experimental condition. For example, the effects of a new speed law in one state were examined by comparing traffic fatalities with neighboring states. The availability of such comparisons provides the researcher with more information about causality than is usually the case with observational research. This is what makes it a quasi-experiment. Of course, drivers could not be assigned at random to different states, so the researchers could only presume that equally safe drivers resided in each state.

2.3. Experimental Design Considerations

A major issue in designing an experiment is whether to use the same or different subjects at each level of the independent variable. *Within-subject manipulations* are those in which each subject receives every level of the independent variable. For that reason, they are sometimes called *repeated-measures* designs. *Between-subjects manipulations* are those in which different subjects receive each level of the independent variable. The main advantage of a within-subject design is that subject characteristics, sometimes called *subject variables* as a parallel term to independent variables, are held constant across experimental conditions. The main advantage of a between-subjects design is that it rules out possible contaminating influences introduced when a subject goes from one experimental condition to another.

2.3.1. Within-Subject Manipulations

The major strength of within-subject manipulations is that they use the same subjects in each experimental condition and thus control for all subject variables. There is no need to be concerned that differences between conditions, for example, in age and gender of the subjects, will have effects that are confused or confounded with the effects of the independent variables. Because every subject serves in every condition of the experiment, all subject variables are guaranteed to be equally distributed over all levels of the independent variable. In other words, subjects in a within-subject design serve as their own controls. Another desirable feature of this design is that it is possible to increase the amount of data provided by each subject and thus reduce the number of subjects needed.

Some studies inherently require repeated measures. A common example of this is the *before-and-after design*. In clinical psychology, the investigator often needs to compare behavior before and after treatment. In political science, the investigator may want to examine how a voter's attitude changes following a particular persuasive communication or an important new event.

The major concern in using within-subject designs is the potential impact of earlier events on later behavior. These are called *carryover effects*. Carryover effects must be controlled to obtain unconfounded measures of the effects of the variables of primary interest. *Counterbalancing* experimental conditions, where, for example, one half of the subjects receive the *AB* sequence and one half receive the *BA* sequence, tends to control progressive changes in behavior such as those produced by practice (a positive effect) or fatigue (a negative effect). The researcher who uses counterbalancing does not eliminate such effects, but strives to distribute them equally across experimental conditions. For example, if performance in condition *B* of a two-task sequence is enhanced because of practice in the sequence *AB*, then performance in condition *A* should be enhanced by approximately the same amount in the sequence *BA*. Then, when *A* and *B* are compared for the combined data for both sequences, these effects will tend to cancel each other out. Furthermore, the use of counterbalanced designs allows the researcher to measure the effects of practice or fatigue by comparing performance in sequences *AB* and *BA*.

Now suppose that the carryover effects differ for different sequences, such as when condition *A* involves the administration of a drug and condition *B* involves the administration of a placebo. When the conditions are given in the *AB* sequence, performance in condition *B* may be influenced by the physiological carryover effects of the drug administered in condition *A*. Even a strong drug effect may go undetected because there might be no differential in performance at the times when conditions *A* and *B* were administered due to the fact that subjects are still being influenced by the drug at the second session. Of course, no such carryover effects occur in the *BA* sequence. In this case, transfer is different in the *AB* and *BA* sequences, and counterbalancing procedures will not solve the problem. A single sequence like *BA* will not suffice either, because then subjects would be more practiced in condition *A* than in condition *B*.

2.3.2. Between-Subjects Manipulations

Between-subjects manipulations are, of course, free of the carryover effects that can complicate or invalidate interpretation of results of within-subject manipulations. Between-subjects manipulations, however, do not have the degree of control over subject variables that within-subject manipulations have. There are, nevertheless, ways to reduce differences between subjects when between-subjects manipulations are used. Subject variables, such as age, gender, and education level, that cannot be manipulated can be controlled through randomization, matching, and selection of homogeneous subject populations.

Matching is a more elaborate way to achieve control of subject variables than complete randomization. If two experimental groups are matched on age, IQ, previous experience, and so forth, then differences between the two groups attributable to different treatment conditions will not be confounded with differences in these subject variables. For example, suppose that subjects were asked whether they favored banning smoking in bars after reading either arguments in favor of the ban (condition *A*), arguments against the ban (condition *B*), or neither (condition *C*). Because attitudes may depend largely on the subject's own history of smoking, it would be logical to first classify the subjects on the basis of whether they are heavy smokers, light smokers, or nonsmokers. Within *each* of these categories, subjects would be assigned at random to conditions *A*, *B*, and *C.* Consequently, one third of the heavy smokers would end up in each condition, one third of the light smokers would end up in each condition, and one-third of the nonsmokers would end up in each condition, thus guaranteeing that the potentially biasing influence of personal smoking history does not contaminate the comparison of conditions *A, B,* and *C* because the subjects in each condition were "matched" on smoking history. Furthermore, the researcher could then compare the influence of the different types of arguments on each type of subject. However, matching serves no useful purpose if the matching factor is not at least moderately correlated with and predictive of the behavior being measured, and one often does not know this until after the study has been conducted. Some information that might be useful for matching purposes, such as IQ scores, may be difficult to obtain and not worth the effort.

2.4. Specific Experimental Designs

2.4.1. Two Independent Random Groups

In the prototypical *independent random groups design,* subjects are assigned to one of two conditions: the experimental condition or the control condition. The subjects in the first group receive some type of experimental treatment (the administration of a drug or therapy, arguments pro or con a particular issue, participation in a group discussion, etc.), whereas subjects in the other group do not receive the treatment. Control is achieved in two ways. First, the two groups are treated alike in all ways (e.g., tested in the same location by the same experimenter) except for the presence or absence of the experimental treatment. In that way, comparison of performance in the two groups will reveal the effect of the treatment.

The second way in which control is achieved is through the use of randomization. Random assignment of subjects to conditions tends to control for subject variables that may confound the results of an experiment if their distribution differs between experimental conditions. Randomization does not guarantee that the effects of subject variables will be equalized across conditions, but it does eliminate systematic sources of bias that would occur if other methods of assignment were used. Assigning subjects to conditions in the order in which they volunteer, for example, could lead to more motivated subjects in some conditions than in others. The larger the sample size and the more homogeneous the sample, the better the expected outcome of randomization because extreme individuals are less apt to be found in a homogeneous sample and less apt to affect the results with a large sample. These points are not only logical from a research design point of view, but, as we will see in the next section, from a statistical point of view as well. The use of homogeneous samples may seem counterintuitive because it limits the generality of results. However, a good research strategy is to maximize the chances of demonstrating an experimental effect by initially focusing on a homogeneous sample and then testing for generality by replicating (repeating) the study with samples from different populations.

2.4.2. More Than Two Independent Random Groups

Many experiments utilize the principles of control described for the two independent random groups design, but require more than two levels of the independent variable. There may be three, four, five, or more levels of an independent variable such as drug dosage and each group of subjects receives a different level.

For two independent random groups, random assignment of subjects to conditions can be accomplished by flipping a coin for each subject. "Heads" means that a subject is assigned to condition A; tails means condition B. For more than two conditions, tossing a die could be used, but a table of random numbers is usually handier. Suppose that a table of random numbers is consulted (see Appendix A) and that the sequence 210732713441116967 is encountered. (Yes, even a set of random numbers can contain three 1s in a row.) If subjects are to be assigned at random to conditions A, B, and C, the following rule could be used: encountering the numbers 1, 2, or 3 leads to assignment to condition A; encountering the numbers 4, 5, or 6 leads to assignment to B; and 7, 8, or 9 leads to C. (The number 0 is skipped.) Following this rule, the first two subjects (e.g., the first two encountered or the first two on an alphabetical list) are assigned to A, the next to condition C, and so forth. When one condition "fills up," for example, 30 of 90 subjects have already been assigned to condition A, then later subjects are assigned only to conditions B and C (i.e., the numbers 1 to 3 are skipped from that point on).

2.4.3. Matched Pairs

The use of matching in a between-subjects design with two groups is called *matched pairs*. In an independent random groups design, the assignment of subjects to one experimental condition is independent of the assignment of subjects to another experimental condition. By contrast, in a matched pairs design, the assignment of a subject to one condition determines the assignment of another subject to the other condition. Matched pairs are formed by taking two subjects with the same or similar values on a subject variable such as age, IQ score, or income, and randomly assigning one member of the pair to one condition and the other to the other condition. For example, a coin flip could be used to determine which of two subjects with identical IQ scores of 125 is assigned to condition *A* and which to condition *B*. Recall that because the two groups are then guaranteed to be equated on that subject variable, that subject variable can be ruled out as a cause of any differences observed later between the two groups.

Randomized blocks design is an extension of the matched pairs design in which subjects are rank ordered on the basis of a numerical subject variable such as scores on a pretest. Subjects are then arranged in blocks corresponding in size to the number of levels of the independent variable. For instance, if there are three levels of the independent variable, the individuals with the top three scores on the pretest would constitute the first block, the next three highest would constitute the second block, and so on. Random assignment of subjects to experimental conditions can then be done separately within each block of subjects. Differences in performance as a function of the blocking variable (pretest score) can be assessed, but, more importantly, such differences can be separated from the effects of the independent variable.

2.4.4. Factorial Designs

Social scientists often include more than one independent variable in a single study. When all possible combinations of levels of the variables are included in the experimental design, it is called a *factorial design*. Such a design not only enables the researcher to examine the separate effects of each variable, but also the *interaction* between variables. The interaction between two variables is a measure of the extent to which the effect of one variable differs at different levels of the other variable. In the classic case of drug interaction, taking one drug affects you differently depending on whether you are taking another particular drug. The interaction effect may well be the most interesting and important finding of such a study.

The logic of the factorial design is simple and can be illustrated in a 3×3 design, where this notation means that there are two independent variables or "factors," each with three levels, and that all nine (3×3) combinations are included in the design. In an example to be developed more fully later, subjects are given varying combinations of dosages of two different drugs. If a between-subjects design is used, then there will be nine separate groups defined as $A_1 B_1$, $A_1 B_2$, $A_1 B_3$, $A_2 B_1$, $A_2 B_2$, $A_2 B_3$, $A_3 B_1$, $A_3 B_2$, and $A_3 B_3$. Recorded responses (dependent variables) can be measures of health status or behavioral reaction. Use of this design eliminates one source of *confounding*—the inability to separate the effects of two or more variables, in this case, A and B. Because levels A_1, A_2, and A_3 are each paired with all levels of B, mean responses across levels of A are not confounded by B. Similarly, because levels B_1, B_2, and B_3 are each paired with all levels of A, comparisons of mean responses across levels of B are not confounded by A. Thus, separate estimates of the effects of each of the two drugs can be obtained in the same experiment as well as the interaction between drugs. The interaction could reveal, for example, that the beneficial effects of both drugs are neutralized when both are taken together in large dosages.

The logic of the factorial design can be extended to a larger number of factors and varying number of levels per factor. The practical limitation is that too many factors and levels yield an unwieldy number of combinations. Partial or *fractional factorial designs* provide a compromise where fewer combinations are needed, but not all effects, especially interactions, can be tested statistically. (See Louviere, 1988, for a more extensive discussion.)

For a more detailed discussion of experimental design considerations and options, see Dominowski (1980), Kantowitz, Roediger, and Elmes (1994), Levin and Hinrichs (1995), and Shaughnessy and Zechmeister (1985).

3. TESTS OF SIGNIFICANCE

This section includes a discussion of tests of statistical significance that provide answers to the questions posed by researchers' hypotheses, as well as a discussion of tests of the strength of relationships revealed through the covariation of measures or events.

3.1. Tests of Statistical Significance: An Overview

Tests of statistical significance provide objective rules for determining whether a researcher's hypotheses are supported by the data. The need for objectivity becomes clear when we realize that the hypotheses refer to values for *populations* of interest, whereas the data come from *samples* of varying reliability in representing the populations. For example, the population of interest may be children aged 4 to 5 and the sample may be children at a particular preschool who are available at the time the data are collected. To conclude that a particular variable influences behavior, the researcher must, of course, follow the principles of good research design described in the preceding section. However, just showing that the scores for an experimental group and a control group are different is not enough. The researcher must also demonstrate that differences in behavior between experimental conditions (e.g., different levels of an independent variable) are reliable; that is, they are greater than differences attributable to chance sampling effects.

Chance sampling effects refer to preexisting differences between samples of individuals that have nothing to do with the treatment they receive in an experiment. Chance sampling effects might be substantial in, say, a study of human behavior where various genetic and environmental factors are beyond the control of the experimenter. As a consequence, researchers typically use randomization as a way to ensure that each subject in an experiment has an equal chance of being assigned to each experimental condition, thus eliminating any systematic bias in the assignment of subjects to conditions. However, as illustrated in Figure 3.1, a *descriptive statistic* such as the sample mean can vary considerably between random samples taken from the same population, especially when sample size is low. This variation is due to the fact that different individuals fall into different samples and each individual has unique characteristics. So, of course the samples will vary one from the other, and the effect of any

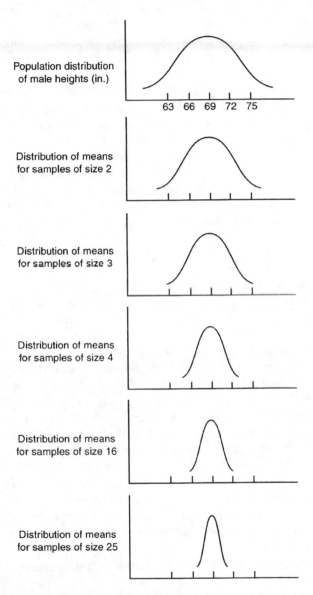

Population distribution
of male heights (in.)

63   66   69   72   75

Distribution of means
for samples of size 2

Distribution of means
for samples of size 3

Distribution of means
for samples of size 4

Distribution of means
for samples of size 16

Distribution of means
for samples of size 25

Figure 3.1. Sampling Distributions for Varying Sample Size

deviant score will be greater for a small sample than for a large one. It then becomes useful to look at the distribution of mean values for different samples. Do the mean values tend to cluster around some central value? How far apart are they? What is the impact of sample size?

The distributions shown in Figure 3.1 are known as *sampling distributions* because they show how a descriptive statistic such as the mean varies or is distributed across repeated random samples from the same population. An important characteristic of sampling distributions of the mean, which is of relevance to the statistical tests described later, is that they tend toward normality as sample size increases, even if the original distribution of scores is not normal. A *normal distribution* is commonly called bell shaped, but it has more precise mathematical properties such as 68% of its scores fall between a point 1 standard deviation unit above the mean and a point 1 standard deviation unit below the mean. Furthermore, as Figure 3.1 clearly shows, the larger the sample size, the less variable will be the sampling distribution, meaning that larger samples produce more precise estimates of population values than do smaller samples. This is because the larger the sample size, the less the mean will be influenced by an extreme score ("outlier"). The measure of variability of a sampling distribution has a special name. It is called the *standard error* and it is calculated as the standard deviation of the sample values (see subsequent text) divided by the square root of the sample size.

The *mean* is an example of a *sample statistic* because it helps summarize the scores in a sample and varies in value from sample to sample. The mean, sometimes called the arithmetic average, is the sum of all the scores divided by the number of scores. Other measures of average do not take into account the exact values of all scores, and thus are less affected by extreme scores. These other measures include the *median*, which is the value of the score that has half the scores above it and half the scores below it, and the *mode*, which is the score that occurs with higher frequency than the other scores in its neighborhood (thus there can be more than one mode in any given set of scores).

Physical measures such as the height of college-age men tend to be normally distributed such that the mean, median, and mode are all approximately equal. However, if we combined men and women in the same set of data, we would likely get a bimodal distribution where the modes tell more about the scores than do the mean or median. Similarly, psychological measures such as scales that measure attitudes toward controversial issues are often bimodal, with individuals having extreme attitudes in either direction. Thus, choosing the best measure to summarize a set of data will depend on how the data are distributed.

The mean has a particular feature that makes it valuable in using sample values to infer values of the population from which it was drawn. The sample mean is an *unbiased estimate* of the population mean, meaning that the mean of a sampling distribution of means computed from repeated random samples of the same size from the same population will equal the population mean. In other words, the distributions shown in Figure 3.1 are centered around the population mean value. Thus, while no single sample mean is likely to precisely duplicate the population mean, there is no systematic tendency for a sample mean to overestimate or underestimate the population mean.

Things are not quite so simple for the sample *standard deviation* as an estimate of the population standard deviation. The standard deviation and its squared value, called the *variance*, are the most common measures of the variability, dispersion, or spread of scores within a set of scores. Information about the spread of scores within a distribution may be equally as important, if not more so, than information about central tendency. For example, two cities may have nearly identical mean high temperatures over the course of a year, but one city may have relatively moderate temperatures all year long, while the other may undergo extreme seasonal changes. Would you want to say that the weather is similar in the two cities? The population standard deviation σ is defined as the square root of the sum of the squared differences between each score X and the mean of the scores μ, divided by the number of scores n; that is,

$$\sigma = \sqrt{\frac{\Sigma(X-\mu)^2}{n}}.$$

In computing the sample standard deviation, s, however, the denominator is changed to $n-1$ because this comes closer to providing an unbiased estimate of the population value; that is,

$$s = \sqrt{\frac{\Sigma (X - \bar{X})^2}{n - 1}},$$

where $\bar{X}$ is the mean of the sample.

To recognize the imprecision inherent in estimating a population value from a single sample, many researchers routinely present an interval of possible values for the population parameter rather than a single point estimate. This is known as a *confidence interval*. For example, consider a sample of size 50 selected at random from a normally distributed population. The 95% confidence interval (CI) for the population mean value is calculated as the mean value obtained from the sample plus or minus 1.96 standard error units, where the standard error is the standard deviation of the sampling distribution. The value 1.96 was selected because 95% of the scores in a normal distribution fall between 1.96 standard deviations above the mean and 1.96 standard deviations below the mean. (Because we are dealing here with sampling distributions, the appropriate standard deviation term is the standard error.) If repeated samples of the same size were selected at random from the same population and the 95% CI was calculated for each sample, then 95% of these CIs would contain the true population mean.

It is the job of *inferential statistics* to provide an estimate of the probability or likelihood that a given set of experimental results was due merely to "chance" factors varying randomly between experimental conditions. When the likelihood of obtaining a set of results by chance is estimated to be very low, the most reasonable conclusion is that the results are due to more than just chance. If the research has been designed and conducted appropriately, the researcher may then conclude that the factor of interest, the independent variable being manipulated, for instance, had a likely effect on behavior.

Herein lie both the strength of the statistical tests and the notes of precaution that must be sounded. The strength, which has been recognized as a major scientific breakthrough, is the establishment of a set of objective decision rules the researcher must adopt to support a scientific claim. We will see a number of examples of such rules in the pages that follow; all should be contrasted with the use of willy-nilly assertions that a particular experimental result is worthy of our attention.

The notes of precaution are simple, but they are often ignored. The statistical tests are quantitative. They yield numbers and people trust numbers (or if they do not understand them, they tend not to question them). The numbers come from data from an experiment. If the experiment is invalid, the numbers will be meaningless. Even the most sophisticated statistical test will not rescue a poorly designed study. The previous section described various methods and principles for creating valid studies. It is of paramount importance for the researcher and the consumer of research to know how the data were collected before taking the numbers too seriously.

3.2. Method of Indirect Proof or Indirect Support

Before we turn to the variety of statistical tests in common use by social scientists, let us briefly describe the underlying logic that guides all these tests, collectively called *hypothesis testing*. Hypothesis testing relies on the so-called *method of indirect proof*, and it is based on the idea that most research questions boil down to two competing hypotheses, with support for one coming from rejection of the other.

The competing hypotheses are referred to as the null hypothesis and the alternative hypothesis. The *null hypothesis* (H_0) is the hypothesis initially assumed to be true. In most cases, H_0 assumes no difference (e.g., the experimental treatment has no effect), whereas the *alternative hypothesis* (H_a) typically affirms the existence of differences among experimental conditions. The null hypothesis does not usually correspond to the actual prediction of the experiment. It is more like a "straw man" that the researcher hopes to discredit. However, because the null hypotheses is stated as an equality (e.g., the difference between the population mean scores of the experimental and control groups is zero) and the alternative hypothesis is stated as an inequality (the difference between the means is not equal to zero), only H_0 can be tested directly, and that is why we start with that hypothesis even though it is not the actual experimental hypothesis. H_0 has a specified numerical value, whereas H_a does not. Examples of null hypotheses include the following statements: a drug has no effect; people are equally persuaded by one-sided and two-sided arguments; individuals will make the same decisions whether they are alone or in groups; men and women have the same tastes in foods. To affirm the existence of a difference or an effect, the researcher must reject or nullify H_0 (that is why it is called the "null" hypothesis) by providing data that are inconsistent with the assumption of no difference. Hence, the term "indirect proof" has been adopted. However, we prefer "indirect support."

Although the first word in the term "indirect proof" clearly describes the logic of hypothesis testing, the second word is an overstatement. It implies that statistical decisions are without error. This is not true. Hypotheses concern population values, but are tested with data from samples, and the correspondence between a sample value and the population it is meant to represent can vary from sample to sample. (See the sampling distributions depicted in Figure 3.1.) Sometimes the mean of a sample of scores will be very close to the population mean (i.e., it will fall near the middle of the sampling distribution) and sometimes it will not (i.e., it will fall in one of the tails of the distribution). The latter cases, although rare, can lead to incorrect decisions. This is shown in Table 3.1.

Errors occur when H_0 is true, but you reject it in favor of H_a, or when H_0 is false, but you retain it. By convention, these two types of errors are called *Type I errors* and *Type II errors*, respectively. The probability of a Type I error (called alpha and denoted α) and the probability of a Type II error (called beta and denoted β) are

TABLE 3.1
Outcomes of Hypothesis Testing

Decision Made	H_0 is Actually	
	True	False
Retain H_0	Correct decision	Type II error (β)
Reject H_0	Type I error (α)	Correct decision (power $P = 1 - \beta$)

inversely related. If a strict criterion is set for rejecting H_0, then H_0 will seldom be rejected when it is true, but H_0 is apt to be retained when it is false, resulting in a low level of alpha and a relatively high level of beta. The opposite occurs with a lax criterion for rejecting H_0. This criterion is called the *level of significance*, which can be set ahead of time as low (e.g., $\alpha = .01$) to reduce the probability of a Type I error or high (e.g., $\alpha = .10$) to reduce the probability of a Type II error. This decision should be based on the judged relative severity of Type I and II errors. For example, when testing the null hypothesis that decisions are the same whether made individually or in groups, a Type I error would mean that the researcher concluded that groups influenced decisions when they actually did not, and a Type II error would mean that the researcher concluded that groups had no influence when they actually did. In medical research, a Type I error could mean that an ineffective drug or treatment was said to have an effect, and a Type II error could mean that a helpful drug or treatment was said to have no effect. Thus, a medical researcher testing the effectiveness of a new drug might want to set $\alpha = .01$ to avoid premature marketing of an unproven drug. In practice, an intermediate level of $\alpha = .05$ is most often used.

Perhaps even more common these days is to incorporate into statistical computer packages the calculation of the *p value* for each statistical computation. This value represents the probability of obtaining a value equal to or more extreme than the computed value of the statistic if the null hypothesis were true; that is, if only "chance" factors were operating. A researcher might then report, for example, that $p = .0778$ for a particular test. The researcher still has to convince the reader that this is a sufficiently small probability to warrant rejection of the null hypothesis and conclude that the results were due to more than just chance.

To accentuate the positive rather than the negative, the probability of correctly rejecting H_0 is called the *power* of a statistical test. This is an important concept because support for the actual experimental hypothesis usually requires rejecting H_0. Although power will decrease when α, the probability of a Type I error, is set low, there are some principles of good experimental design that can be used to increase power for detecting a difference between experimental conditions: keep sample size large; select homogeneous subject populations; use repeated measures on the same subjects; use standardized and unambiguous tasks, instructions, and response measures.

Now we briefly describe the most common statistical tests used in hypothesis testing. Later we provide more detailed examples of their use.

3.3. Statistical Tests for Two Means: The t Test

The t test is most often used to compare the means of two experimental conditions. Two applications can be distinguished. The first one applies to experiments with two independent groups such as when subjects are assigned at random to an experimental group and a control group. The null hypothesis is that the population mean scores are equal for the two conditions. In other words, no difference would be found if we could compare the entire population of scores for the experimental and control conditions, H_0: $\mu_E - \mu_C = 0$, where μ_E and μ_C represent the population mean values for the experimental and control conditions, respectively. The alternative hypothesis is that a difference would be found, H_a: $\mu_E - \mu_C \neq 0$. (If the direction of difference were predicted ahead of time, a "one-tailed" version of H_a would be specified such as $\mu_E - \mu_C > 0$. This will be illustrated shortly.)

The test assumes that the distribution of scores in each condition is normal and that the two distributions have equal variance. There is considerable evidence, however, that the t test is relatively unaffected by moderate deviations from these assumptions when sample sizes are equal. (Recall that sampling distributions of the mean tend to be normal even if the population from which samples are drawn is nonnormal.) According to Gardner (1975), the most serious violations are when different samples are drawn from populations with widely different shaped distributions or when samples of unequal size have different variances. The following values are computed for the two samples of scores obtained in the experiment: the means, $\overline{X}_E$ and $\overline{X}_C$, the standard deviations, s_E and s_C, and the sample sizes, n_E and n_C. (Note that Greek letters are often used to denote population values and Latin letters are used to denote sample values. This is done to clearly distinguish population from sample. Hypotheses are stated for the populations of interest; they are tested with data from samples.) The value of t is then computed using the formula

$$t = \left(\overline{X}_E - \overline{X}_C \right) / \sqrt{\left(\frac{(n_E - 1) s_E^2 + (n_C - 1) s_C^2}{n_E + n_C - 2} \right) \left(\frac{n_E + n_C}{n_E n_C} \right)},$$

which simplifies to

$$t = \frac{\overline{X}_E - \overline{X}_C}{\sqrt{(s_E^2 + s_C^2)/n}}$$

for the case of equal sample size, $n_E - n_C = n$.

The resulting value of t is then compared with the *critical value* found in a table of the t statistic (see Appendix B) using the selected level of α and the appropriate *degrees of freedom*, $df = (n_E - 1) + (n_C - 1)$. The degrees of freedom for a particular sample are $(n - 1)$, because once we know the mean of that sample, we only need to know $(n - 1)$ scores and then the last score can be automatically determined. The critical value defines that portion of the tail or tails of the distribution of t that represents an area equal to α. This area is called the *critical region*. Because degrees of freedom are related to sample size and because larger samples produce more reliable results, the critical value decreases as df increases. If the absolute value of t calculated from the data is larger than the value in the table, then the decision is to reject H_0 in favor of H_a. Otherwise, H_0 is retained. This will be illustrated in the next section.[3]

We can distinguish here between *one-tailed* and *two-tailed* tests. For $\alpha = .05$ and a one-tailed test where H_a: $\mu_E - \mu_C > 0$, the critical region is the upper tail of the distribution and it takes a large positive value of t to reject H_0 in favor of H_a. For H_a: $\mu_E - \mu_C < 0$, the critical region is the lower tail of the distribution, and it takes a large negative value of t to reject H_0 in favor of H_a. An example of H_a: $\mu_E - \mu_C > 0$ would be comparing the reduction in clinical symptoms between a group receiving a particular treatment and a group not receiving the treatment (e.g., a placebo group). Because the treatment would be supported only if it were *better than* no treatment, this particular one-tailed test would be appropriate. Note, however, that we would then fail to distinguish between an ineffective treatment and a harmful one, which is all right as long as we discontinue use of a treatment in either of these cases. Otherwise, a two-tailed test would be more appropriate. An example of H_a: $\mu_E - \mu_C < 0$ would be comparing the number of correct responses in recalling a list by a group of subjects who had learned a prior interfering list with the number of correct responses by a control group who had not learned the prior list. Interference theory *predicts* that the experimental group will perform worse; hence a one-tailed test. For $\alpha = .05$ and a two-tailed test (with no a priori predictions) where H_a: $\mu_E - \mu_C \neq 0$, the critical region is divided into two parts: the upper 2.5% of the curve and the lower 2.5% of the curve. Either a large positive value of t or a large negative value of t can lead to rejection of H_0. Because the total area of the critical region is the same for one-tailed and two-tailed tests, it takes a larger absolute value of t to attain significance with a two-tailed test. That is, given the same sample data reflecting a difference between sample means, the value of t is more apt to fall into the critical region for a one-tailed test than for a two-tailed test. In other words, one-tailed tests have more power than two-tailed tests. This is shown in Figure 3.2.

If the calculated absolute value of t is less than the value in the table, then H_0 must be retained as a viable option. The rationale in the case of retaining H_0 is that the observed difference is not sufficient in magnitude to conclude that the two conditions are different. The rationale in the case of rejecting H_0 is that the observed difference between the means of the two samples is too great to be attributable to chance, so the researcher concludes that scores for the experimental and control groups are truly different. This is often referred to as a *statistically significant difference*.[4]

For some researchers, the *size* of the effect is more important than whether or not it achieves a particular level of significance. Even an effect that is "statistically significant" may be too small in magnitude to have much "practical significance." Furthermore, researchers using a technique known as *meta-analysis* have used *effect size* as their unit of analysis for testing reliability of research results by combining the data from all known studies of the effect. Meta-analysis also allows the investigator to uncover factors such as subject variables that account for differences in results between studies. The interested reader is referred to Hedges, Shymansky, and Woodworth (1989) for a more complete description of this method and to Smith

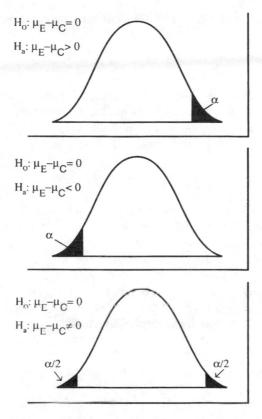

Figure 3.2. The Critical Regions for One-Tailed and Two-Tailed Tests

and Glass (1977) for an illustration of its application to the study of the effectiveness of psychotherapy.

The second application of the t test refers to comparisons of means of matched pairs of scores, such as when the same individuals are tested before and after some experimental treatment. Here the competing hypotheses can be stated as H_0: $\mu_D = 0$ and H_a: $\mu_D \neq 0$ (or $\mu_D < 0$ or $\mu_D > 0$ for one-tailed tests), where μ_D is the mean of the population of *difference scores*. In compiling the sample data, a difference score is calculated for each pair of scores and the following values are tabulated: the number of pairs, n; the mean difference between pairs within the sample, $\overline{D}$; and the standard deviation of the difference scores, s_D. The value of t is then computed from the formula

$$t = \overline{D}/(s_D/\sqrt{n}).$$

Again, the computed value of t is compared to the "critical value" in the table, this time using $(n - 1)$ as the degrees of freedom. If the computed value of t is larger than the value in the table, H_0 is rejected in favor of H_a; otherwise, H_0 is retained.

3.4. Statistical Tests for More Than Two Means: Analysis of Variance

As with the t test, we distinguish two versions of the analysis of variance (ANOVA) and its associated statistic, the F test. The first version is called *one-way ANOVA* because there is only one independent variable, but it may have a number of different levels, as when you are comparing various dosages of a drug or varying amounts of reinforcement. The null hypothesis here is H_0: $\mu_1 = \mu_2 = \cdots = \mu_k$, where μ_i is the population mean for level i. The alternative hypothesis states that the population means are not all equal.

One-way analysis of variance is like an extension of the t test, but recall that t tests can compare only two means at a time. If, for example, there were 8 groups to be compared and you used t to compare every possible pair, you would have to conduct 28 different t tests. (28 is the number of combinations of 8 things taken 2 at a time.) If each individual t test is conducted with $\alpha = .05$, it is simple to see that 28 such tests could easily lead to one or more Type I errors because the expected number of such errors is $28 \times 0.05 = 1.40$. A single analysis of variance is preferred on the grounds that it does not inflate the likelihood of making a Type I error.

The F test used in ANOVA is defined as the ratio of two sample variances, that is, $F = s_1^2/s_2^2$; hence the term, "analysis of variance." In the case of one-way ANOVA, the variance term in the numerator is called *between-groups variance* because it is a measure of how much the k different group means vary from each other. The variance term in the denominator is called *within-group variance* because it is a measure of the average variance of scores within each experimental condition. The denominator is thus a measure of *sampling error*, the extent of difference due merely to chance factors. The numerator is a measure that includes sampling error plus any differences between experimental conditions that go beyond sampling error. The larger the ratio of between-groups variance to within-group variance, the less likely that the null hypothesis is true. The logic here is that if H_0 were true, then the numerator and denominator would each measure sampling error and thus the ratio would be approximately 1.0, but if H_0 were false, then the numerator contains one more component than the denominator and thus the ratio would be greater than 1.0. In other words, the F test measures the extent to which differences in scores between different groups of subjects are greater than differences within a single group. Like t, the F test assumes normal distributions with equal variances for each separate group.

Computational formulas for one-way ANOVA are summarized in Table 3.2, which also shows the typical format for presenting results.

In ANOVA terms, the F test translates into the formula

$$F = \frac{\text{MS between groups}}{\text{MS within groups}},$$

where MS denotes mean squares.

"Mean squares" (MS) is an appropriate statistical term for variances because variance is calculated as the mean of the squared deviations of each score from the mean of the scores. "Sum of

TABLE 3.2

Computational Formulas for One-Way Analysis of Variance (ANOVA)

Source of Variance	df	Sum of Squares (SS)	Mean Square (MS)
Between groups	$(k - 1)$	$\sum_{j=1}^{k} \dfrac{T_j^2}{n} - \dfrac{T^2}{N}$	$SS_{\text{between}}/(k - 1)$
Within groups	$k(n - 1)$	$SS_{\text{total}} - SS_{\text{between}}$	$SS_{\text{within}}/k(n - 1)$
Total	$N - 1$	$\sum_{j=1}^{k} \sum_{i=1}^{n} X_{ij}^2 - \dfrac{T^2}{N}$	

Notes: k = number of groups; n = number of subjects per group; $N = kn$ = total number of subjects; T_j = sum or total of scores in group j; T = sum of scores in all groups; X_{ij} = the score for the ith subject in group j; $\sum_{j=1}^{k} \sum_{i=1}^{n} X_{ij}^2$ = sum of squared scores for all subjects in all groups. The statistic for testing H_0 is the F test, where F = MS between groups/MS within groups.

squares" (SS) is the statistical term for the numerator of a variance that is included for computational ease. Of course, modern computer technology can bypass this step. The calculated value of F is compared with a "critical value" found in a table of F distributions (see Appendix C), using the selected level of α and the appropriate degrees of freedom, in this case separate degrees of freedom terms for the numerator and denominator. Following the same logic as with t, H_0 is rejected when the value of F computed from the data exceeds the critical value in the table; otherwise, H_0 is retained. Because variances must be positive and the calculation of F involves squaring all differences, F cannot take on negative values and, unlike t, the critical region is always in the upper tail of the distribution. When H_0 is rejected, researchers can conduct additional tests to localize the inequality or to examine the trends exhibited in the data. These additional tests typically adjust for inflated rates of Type I error by taking into account the number of means to be compared. Such tests will be illustrated later.

The illustration in Table 3.2 was for a between-subjects design, where a different sample of subjects received each of the k levels of the independent variable. One-way ANOVA can also be applied to the data from a within-subject design, where each subject receives each of the k levels of the independent variable. The computational formulas here are different from those for the between-subjects design because differences in response as a function of different levels of the independent variable (the numerator term of the F ratio) are compared to a new measure of "sampling error" (the denominator of the F ratio): differences due to chance between repeated measures on the same subjects. These computational formulas can be found in many statistics texts such as Hays (1994).

The second type of ANOVA is called *multifactor ANOVA* because it deals with more than one variable in a study using a factorial design. Analogous to one-way ANOVA, multifactor ANOVA includes a separate F test for each variable. For example, if there are two factors A and B, and each factor has three levels with all nine possible combinations included in the experimental design, then separate F tests are conducted for the two null hypotheses H_0: $\mu_{A1} = \mu_{A2} = \mu_{A3}$, corresponding to comparison of population means for the three levels of A, averaged over levels of B, and H_0: $\mu_{B1} = \mu_{B2} = \mu_{B3}$, corresponding to comparison of population means for the three levels of B, averaged over levels of A. These are called tests of *main effects*, and the logic behind the use of the F test is the same as for one-way ANOVA. In addition, a new concept is introduced: the *interaction* between variables. In this case, a separate null hypothesis is tested. In words, the hypothesis of no interaction states that the effect of variable A should be the same at each level of variable B and vice versa. The alternate hypothesis is that there is an interaction where the effect of each variable differs at different levels of the other variable. Examples of interactions include the following situations: of two alternative treatments for depression, one is more effective for woman and the other for men; the effects of varying the amount of reward for rats running to the end of a maze are greater for those who had been deprived of food for 20 hours than for those who had been deprived of food for 5 hours; increases in heart rate for increasing amounts of exercise are greater for smokers than for nonsmokers.

Computational formulas and presentation format for multifactor ANOVA are summarized in Table 3.3 for the two variable case, called two-way ANOVA, in which both variables are manipulated between subjects; that is, a different group of subjects is used for each of the nine $A \times B$ combinations. An example of this type will be worked out in detail in the next section, where the variables A and B correspond to dosages of two different drugs and the emphasis is determining whether there is a drug interaction effect. As with one-way ANOVA, variations of these formulas apply to within-subject manipulations, including "mixed" designs, where one variable is manipulated between subjects, with a different sample of subjects at each level, and another variable is manipulated within subjects, with the same subjects receiving each level.

Each calculated F ratio is then compared to the appropriate "critical value" in the table of the F distribution. When the interaction test is significant, it is particularly important to describe and understand its nature. As will be shown in the later illustration, a graphic representation of the interaction can be particularly illuminating.

3.5. Statistical Tests for Frequency Distributions: χ^2

Whereas t and F are used to test hypotheses about mean score values, chi-square (χ^2) is used to test hypotheses about the frequency with which subjects' responses fall into different categories. Sample data are in the form of "counts" of observations in each of

TABLE 3.3

Computational Formulas for Two-Factor ANOVA[5]

Source of Variance	df	Sum of Squares (SS)	Mean Square (MS)
Row variable (R)	$(r - 1)$	$\dfrac{\sum\limits_{j=1}^{r} T_{R_j}^2}{cn} - \dfrac{T^2}{N}$	$\dfrac{SS_R}{r - 1}$
Column variable (C)	$(c - 1)$	$\dfrac{\sum\limits_{k=1}^{c} T_{C_k}^2}{rn} - \dfrac{T^2}{N}$	$\dfrac{SS_C}{c - 1}$
Interaction ($R \times C$)	$(r - 1)(c - 1)$	$\dfrac{\sum T_{jk}^2}{n} - \dfrac{T^2}{N} - SS_R - SS_C$	$\dfrac{SS_{R \times C}}{(r - 1)(c - 1)}$
Within group	$rc(n - 1)$	$SS_{total} - SS_R - SS_C - SS_{R \times C}$	$\dfrac{SS_{within}}{rc(n - 1)}$
Total	$N - 1$	$\sum\limits_{k=1}^{c} \sum\limits_{j=1}^{r} \sum\limits_{i=1}^{n} X_{jk}^2 - \dfrac{T^2}{N}$	

Notes: r = number of rows; c = number of columns; n = number of subjects per cell; $N = rcn$ = total number of subjects; T_{R_j} = sum of scores in row j; T_{C_k} = sum of scores in column k; T_{jk} = sum of scores in the cell formed by the intersection of row j and column k; T = sum of scores in all cells of the design; X_{jk} = the score for the ith subject in the cell formed by the intersection of row j and column k; $\sum\limits_{k=1}^{c} \sum\limits_{j=1}^{r} \sum\limits_{i=1}^{n} X_{jk}^2$ = sum of squared scores for all subjects in all cells.

several outcome categories, where each observation can fall into one and only one category and the categories are mutually exclusive and exhaustive. Such data are called *nominal data* because they merely name the category to which an observation belongs. For example, each voter in a political poll designed to predict the outcome of an election can vote for only one candidate, the different candidates represent the different categories into which a response can fall, and the data are summarized by indicating the total number of votes in the sample for each candidate. The null hypothesis is that the number of voters in the population favoring each candidate is the same. Calculation of χ^2 uses the formula

$$\chi^2 = \sum_{i=1}^{k} \left[\frac{(O_i - E_i)^2}{E_i} \right],$$

where k is the number of categories, O_i is the observed frequency in category i, and E_i is the expected frequency if the null hypothesis were true. If there were 4 candidates and 100 voters in the sample, then the expected frequencies under the assumption of no preference (H_0) would be 25 for each candidate. If one candidate received, say, 40 votes, that would be sufficient to conclude that the candidates are not equally preferred. (An extended example, adding gender of the voter as a variable, will be developed in the next section.) As with the t test and F test, H_0 is rejected in favor of H_a (the frequencies are not equal) when the calculated value of χ^2 exceeds the "critical" value in the table of the χ^2 distribution for the designated level of α and degrees of freedom (in this case, the number of categories, k, minus 1 because, by knowing the total number of subjects, we only need the frequencies in $k - 1$ categories and we can get the last one by subtracting). [A rule of thumb for using the χ^2 table is that for more than a single degree of freedom, a minimum expected frequency of 5 is required in each category; for a single degree of freedom, 10 is suggested (Hays, 1994).] Like F, χ^2 cannot be negative because it sums squared values and thus the critical region is always in the upper tail of the distribution.

3.6. Statistical Tests for Relationships: Correlation and Regression

We now move from tests of statistical significance, which lead to decisions concerning whether or not a variable has an effect, to tests that assess the association between variables and quantify the strength of relationship between variables.

Correlation is a way to quantify the relationship between paired scores and *regression* is a way to use this information to predict values of one of the scores. For example, a psychologist might be interested in the relationship between amount of therapy and degree of recovery from depression, and predicting how much improvement can be expected following a given amount of therapy.

3.6.1. Correlation

Only the case of *linear relationships* will be considered; that is, situations where a *scatter diagram* plotting each pair of values (e.g., X_1, Y_1, for individual 1) as a point in two-dimensional space has the form of an ellipse with a straight line providing "the line of best fit" to the points within the ellipse. When the variables are linearly related, Pearson's correlation coefficient r is a measure of the degree of relationship present. In addition to linearity, there are other assumptions underlying the appropriateness of using r as the measure of association between two variables. For example, the standard deviation of the Y scores should be the same for each value of X. The references cited at the end of this section describe these assumptions in more detail. The formula for r is

$$r = \sum_{i=1}^{n} Z(X_i)Z(Y_i)/n,$$

where $Z(X_i)$ and $Z(Y_i)$ are the *standard score transformations* of the scores X_i and Y_i, respectively, and n is the number of paired observations of X and Y. The standard score transformation [e.g., $Z(X_i) = (X_i - \overline{X})/s_X$] expresses each score in units of standard deviations (s_X) from the sample mean $(\overline{X})$ rather than in physical units, so a correlation between, say, body temperature and blood pressure, will be the same if the measures are expressed in metric units or in U.S. customary units. The formula can then be stated simply as the mean of the cross product of standard scores.

In addition to being unit-free, the correlation coefficient has the desirable property that it is bounded by $+1$ [for a perfect positive correlation, where $Z(Y) = Z(X)$ for each pair of values] and -1 [for a perfect negative correlation, where $Z(Y) = -Z(X)$ for each pair], with $r = 0$ representing no relationship between the variables. If $r = \pm 1$, all points will fall on a straight line; if $r = 0$, the points will form a circular array. For intermediate values of r, an ellipse will be formed. The higher the absolute value of r, the "tighter" will be the ellipse and the closer the points will be to a straight line. This is illustrated in Figure 3.3. The value of r is constrained by the variability of the X and Y scores. If either or both of these variables show little variation across observations, then there is little room to show a relationship between X and Y, and r will be low. For example, the correlation between high school grade point average and scores on a college entrance exam is apt to be lower for students at a highly selective college than for other colleges, because all the students at the select college will score high on both measures.

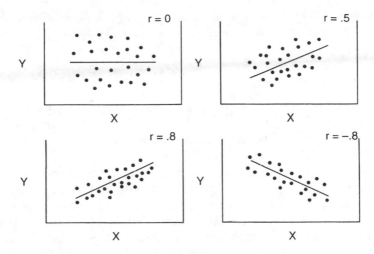

Figure 3.3. Scatterplots for Correlations of Varying Magnitude

3.6.2. Regression

A graphical description also indicates the relationship between correlation and prediction. If the scatter diagram of paired values of X and Y is used to predict the value of Y for a new value of X, then the *regression line* will give the best prediction. This is defined as the line that gives the "best fit" in the sense that the sum of the squared deviations of the Y values from this line is less than from any other straight line. The less the scatter or variability of points around the line—that is, the higher the absolute value of r—the more accurate the prediction. This can be seen most clearly in Figure 3.3 by comparing the panel for $r = .8$ with the panel for $r = 0$. In each case, pick a value of X along the abscissa and use the regression line to predict the value of Y for that value of X. The predicted value of Y will, on average, be much closer to the actual data points for $r = .8$ than for $r = 0$. The stronger the relationship, the greater the extent to which knowing X reduces our uncertainty about Y, as illustrated in the figure. The standard score form of the formula for the regression line is simply $Z(Y) = rZ(X)$. This formula states that when X and Y are expressed in standard scores, then the regression line passes through the origin, with slope equal to r. With this formula (or its computational equivalent using raw scores to be illustrated later), Y can be predicted for any X. The higher the absolute value of r, the more accurate, on average, will be this prediction.

3.6.3. Multiple Regression

If a variable Y can be predicted from a single variable that is known to be correlated with Y, then it stands to reason that better predictions of Y can be made from several variables that are correlated with Y. The *multiple regression equation*, $Y = a + b_1 X_1 + b_2 X_2 + \cdots + b_k X_k$, predicts the value of Y for any combination of values of the variables $X_1, X_2, \ldots, X_k$. In the equation, a is the intercept and $b_1, b_2, \ldots, b_k$ are coefficients that correspond to the weights or contributions of each of the X variables. When $k = 1$, the formula reduces to the simple regression case described previously. Corresponding to r in the single-variable case is the multiple correlation coefficient, R, which is the correlation between the observed values of Y and the predicted values of Y based on the equation. The square of the multiple correlation coefficient, R^2, is a measure of the percentage of variance in Y accounted for by the Xs, corresponding to the reduction in the amount of uncertainty in predicting Y by virtue of knowing the Xs in the equation. Computational formulas (translated into computer programs) have been developed to find the values of $a, b_1, b_2, \ldots, b_k$ that will result in the highest possible correlation between the observed and predicted values of Y. Because there is no guarantee that the relationship between Y and the Xs is actually linear, a linear regression analysis will not necessarily lead to a good fit. Hypothesis testing procedures are available to test the significance of the combined effects of several variables, as well as to test the significance of the incremental effect of adding each X variable.

A variety of textbooks and monographs provide more detailed descriptions of the tests described in this section; in some cases they include more formal distinctions than those used here. For example, the "error term" (denominator of the F test) in ANOVA is different for within-subject and between-subjects variables, and the calculations differ with equal sample size per experimental condition and unequal sample size. Standard statistical computer packages allow the user to specify which variables are repeated measures and which are between subjects. A distinction is also made between the "fixed effects model" of analysis of variance and the "random effects model." In the fixed effects model, the researcher is only interested in making inferences about differences among the levels of the variable actually administered in the study; in the random effects model, the researcher considers the variable levels as random samples of levels of that variable and is interested in making inferences about the entire population of factor levels, not just those actually observed. Most of our examples fall under the category of fixed effects, but see Jackson and Brashers (1994) for more on random effects ANOVA.

Among the "classic" comprehensive statistics textbooks that have gone through several editions are Edwards (1968), Hays (1994), Kirk (1982), and Winer, Brown, and Michels (1991). Some recent "basic" statistics books include Harris (1998) and Hopkins, Hopkins, and Glass, (1996). In addition, the current Sage Series on Quantitative Applications in the Social Sciences includes the following titles for expanded discussion of specific issues in statistics: *Analysis of Variance*, 2nd ed., by Iversen and Norpoth; *Tests of Significance* by Henkel; *Applied Regression* by Lewis-Beck; *Measures of Association* by Liebetrau; *Understanding Regression Analysis* by Schroeder, Sjoquist, and Stephan; *Understanding Significance Testing* by Mohr; *Experimental Design and Analysis* by Brown and Melamed.

4. MATCHING RESEARCH DESIGNS AND STATISTICAL TESTS

In this section we consider the research designs and measures described in Section 2 and illustrate, in diverse examples, the application of the appropriate statistical tests from Section 3. The goal is to provide easy to remember prototypes of application of each statistical test which can be related to new examples that arise in various research settings. We start by describing the role played by the response measure (dependent variable) in determining which statistical analyses are appropriate.

4.1. Response Measures and Statistical Tests

The nature of the response measures is an important component of the research design used to select appropriate statistical tests. For example, in a study using the experimental method, if a categorical response measure is used (e.g., whether or not the subject completes the experimental task in the time allotted or whether or not a subject takes the side advocated by a particular persuasive message), then the χ^2 test will be used to compare responses across experimental conditions. If the response scale is continuous and measures the arithmetic magnitude of some variable (e.g., the amount of time required to complete the task, or the number of errors made, or the rated strength of endorsement of a particular issue), then a t test or analysis of variance would be used, depending on the number of independent variables and levels.

The count or frequency data used in χ^2 tests can be considered as examples of the *nominal scale* of measurement because they need include no more information than naming the category to which a response belongs. In contrast, the continuous data used in t tests and F tests are examples of *interval scales*, because they tell us about the magnitude of difference between scores, or *ratio scales*, that have a true zero value and can thus tell us about the ratio as well as the difference between scores. In the physical world, height and weight are examples of ratio scales, whereas temperature in degrees Fahrenheit is an interval scale. There is also an intermediate category called the *ordinal scale* of measurement, which often comes up in the social sciences. Data from such scales tell us more than the nominal category into which a particular response falls: they indicate when one response represents a higher amount of some variable than another. Some responses obtained in social science research are inherently of this nature such as when subjects are asked to rank order a series of objects or assign them to categories like "above average," "average," and "below average," which imply an *order relation*. With this kind of data, algebraic differences between values are often meaningless. For example, we cannot say that the difference in perceived quality between the object ranked first and the object ranked second is the same as the difference between the object ranked second and the object ranked third. Such data may be analyzed with nonparametric tests that do not merely categorize responses (as with χ^2), but take into account ranked or ordered values. (See Siegel and Castellan, 1988, for a comprehensive description of nonparametric tests for the behavioral sciences.) A commonly used test, the Mann–Whitney test, will be illustrated later.

The distinction between ordinal and interval scales, however, is often not sharp in social science research. Take the case of measuring attitudes using rating scales. In rating one's attitude toward three different objects, one may be able to convey not only that X_1 is preferred over X_2 and that X_2 is preferred over X_3, but also that X_2 is closer to X_1 than it is to X_3. In other words, the scale of measurement may be somewhere between an ordinal and an interval scale. A number of authors have suggested that treating data of this kind as if they had interval properties (i.e., that parametric tests such as t and ANOVA could be applied) would be unlikely to lead to improper conclusions (Gardner, 1975; McNemar, 1969). Parametric tests are commonly applied to such data.

The type of relationship that different methods focus on is also important in selecting statistical tests. On the face of it, it appears that the method of observation, because it focuses on relationships between freely varying factors in the real world, relies on correlation and regression as its principal statistical tools. The experimental method, because it compares behavioral measures across discrete levels of independent variables, relies primarily on t tests, χ^2, and analysis of variance. In many cases, these generalizations hold true, but there are exceptions. For example, an observational study might examine the relationship between a continuous variable like the amount of money spent on a shopping trip and a dichotomous subject characteristic such as the gender of the shopper. A t test comparing the average expenditure of female and male shoppers would be in order here. Many applications of the experimental method include demographic characteristics of the subjects or their scores on survey scales that reflect previous experience, mood, and the like. In such cases, combinations of regression and analysis of variance may be in order.

4.2. Comparison of Two Sample Means

Recall that t tests are used to test hypotheses about the equality of two sample means. Applications include the *two independent random groups design* and the *matched pairs design*. In each case the response measure is continuous and each of the two response distributions to be compared is assumed to be approximately normal and each is assumed to have approximately equal variance.

4.2.1. t-Test for Independent Groups

The prototype of the two independent random groups design involves a comparison between an experimental group and a control group. Let us say that a sample of 8-year-old boys is randomly divided in half, each half assigned to one of the following two conditions: an experimental condition where the boys are exposed to a 30-min video of some of the most violent scenes from the leading action–adventure television series of the season; and a control condition where the boys are exposed to 30-min of nonviolent television. (*Precautionary note*: Material for the control must be selected to be of approximately the same interest level as material for the experimental condition; otherwise, violence level and interest level would be confounded.) Subjects in each group are then put into a play situation where an observer records aggressive behavior by watching the boys through a one-way mirror. It is important here for the recording of aggressive acts to be unbiased. The same "shove" could be viewed as a playful act by one judge and as an act of aggression by another judge. Therefore, the judge should be carefully trained in scoring behavior and should probably be "blind" as to which condition each boy is in.

Box 4.1 illustrates calculations and hypothesis tests for this example. In this hypothetical case, the calculated value of t exceeds the critical value for the appropriate degrees of freedom and level of significance. The conclusion is then that the null hypothesis of no

---

Box 4.1. Application of t Test for Two Independent Random Groups Design

Independent variable manipulation: A sample of 8-year-old boys is randomly assigned to a violent TV condition and a nonviolent TV condition.

Dependent variable measure: Number of aggressive acts in a play situation.

Null hypothesis: The mean number of aggressive acts is the same in the violent (V) and nonviolent (NV) conditions. H_0: $\mu_V - \mu_{NV} = 0$, where the population means, μ_V and μ_{NV}, are compared. (Recall the earlier discussion regarding the lack of specificity in defining the parent population when a "handy" sample is selected.)

Alternative hypothesis: The mean number of aggressive acts is greater in condition V than in condition NV. H_a: $\mu_V - \mu_{NV} > 0$.

Data compilation: The relevant summary data are the number of subjects in each condition, the mean score in each condition, and the standard deviation of scores in each condition.

Condition	n	$\overline{X}$	s
V	25	5.3	2.5
NV	25	3.4	2.0

Calculation of t:

$$t = \frac{\overline{X}_V - \overline{X}_{NV}}{\sqrt{s_V^2/n_V + s_{NV}^2/n_{NV}}} = \frac{5.3 - 3.4}{\sqrt{(2.5)^2/25 + (2.0)^2/25}} = 2.97.$$

Critical value: The table of critical values of t is given in Appendix B. For $\alpha = .05$ and $df = (25 - 1) + (25 - 1) = 48$ with a one-tailed test, the critical value of t is 1.68. This value is determined by looking at the column for $P = .05$ (one-tailed) and the row corresponding to $df = 48$ in the table of the distribution of t. Because there is no row for 48 exactly, interpolation is used to come up with a value between the tabled values for $df = 40$ and $df = 60$, and then the number is rounded off to two decimal places.

Decision: Reject H_0 in favor of the alternative hypothesis that the mean number of aggressive acts is greater in the violent TV condition than in the nonviolent TV condition.

We can now take the further step of using the sample data to compute a 95% confidence interval for the population mean difference, $\mu_V - \mu_{NV}$. In the case of the difference between two means, this confidence interval is calculated as the difference between the two sample means (numerator of the equation for t) ± 2.01 times the standard error (denominator of the equation for t). The value of 2.01 comes from the t table, interpolating a value for $df = 48$ and using $P = .05$, two-tailed because you want to build an interval above and below the sample

Box 4.1. (*Continued*)

mean difference. (This value is slightly different from the value of 1.96 mentioned earlier in the text; that value was based on using the table for a normal distribution rather than the t table, which is more appropriate for the present case.) Hence,

$$95\% \text{ CI} = 1.90 \pm 2.01 \times .64 = 1.90 \pm 1.28.$$

In words, the 95% confidence interval for the population mean difference is the range of values 0.62 to 3.18.

---

difference between experimental and control conditions is rejected in favor of the alternative hypothesis that the mean number of aggressive acts is greater in the experimental condition than in the control condition. If the experimenter is confident that all potential extraneous variables were controlled, that is, held constant across conditions, then he or she can conclude that the different levels of aggression exhibited in the experimental and control conditions were caused by the amount of violent television viewed prior to the measurement of aggression.

4.2.2. t-Test for Repeated Measures or Matched Pairs

A repeated measures design or a matched pairs design could also be applied to the preceding problem. First, consider the repeated measures design. Here, each boy would come back twice, once to view 30 min of violent television and once to view 30 min of nonviolent television. Aggressive behavior would be measured after each session. In compiling the data for such an experiment, the same subject's scores in the two experimental conditions would form a "matched pair." Many precautions are needed to implement this design. Counterbalancing is needed where a randomly selected half of the boys receive the conditions in the order experimental condition then control condition, and the other half receive the conditions in the opposite order. The two sessions would be spaced far enough apart, perhaps a week, to avoid having the boys recall how they behaved the first time. Data analysis is illustrated in Box 4.2, where

Box 4.2. Application of t Test for Repeated Measures Design

Independent variable manipulation: Each boy receives both the experimental (violent TV) and control (nonviolent TV) conditions at different times. A randomly selected half of the boys receive the conditions in the order V and NV, and the other half receive the conditions in the order NV and V.

Dependent variable measure: Number of aggressive acts in a play situation, measured twice for each subject, once following each experimental session.

Null hypothesis: The mean difference in number of aggressive acts between the two sessions for a given subject is zero. H_0: $\mu_D = 0$, where μ_D is the mean difference score for the population.

Alternative hypothesis: When the number of aggressive acts in condition NV is subtracted from the number of aggressive acts in condition V for each subject, the mean difference will be greater than zero. H_a: $\mu_D > 0$.

Data compilation: A difference score is computed for each subject; it represents the algebraic difference (retaining the sign) in number of aggressive acts between conditions V and NV; that is, $d = X_V - X_{NV}$. The relevant summary data are the number of difference scores (i.e., the number of subjects), the mean difference score, and the standard deviation of the difference scores:

$$n = 50, \qquad \bar{d} = 1.9, \qquad s_D = 1.5.$$

Calculation of t:

$$t = \frac{\bar{d}}{s_D/\sqrt{n}} = \frac{1.9}{1.5/\sqrt{50}} = 8.95.$$

Critical value: From Appendix B, for $\alpha = .05$ and $df = (50 - 1) = 49$, the critical value of t is 1.68 for a one-tailed test.

Decision: Reject H_0 in favor of the alternative hypothesis that the mean difference in the number of aggressive acts between the violent and nonviolent TV conditions is greater than zero. Note that the standard error (denominator) term here is smaller than the comparable term in Box 4.1. Although these data are fictitious, this would be the expected outcome of comparing a within-subject design with a between-subjects design.

Calculation of 95% confidence interval for population mean difference score:

$$95\% \text{ CI} = \bar{d} \pm 2.01 s_D/\sqrt{n} = 1.90 \pm 2.01 \times .21 = 1.48 \text{ to } 2.32.$$

the unit of analysis is the difference between the same boy's aggression scores in the two different conditions.

Now consider a matched pairs design for the same situation illustrated in Box 4.2. Instead of assigning the boys at random to the two different conditions of violent and nonviolent TV viewing, the researcher obtains prior information about each boy's aggressive tendencies by interviewing teachers, parents, and peers. The boys are then rank ordered on a composite measure of the data obtained from the interviews. The top two boys are assigned at random to the two different conditions, for example, by flipping a coin. The same is done for each successive pair. The result is that prior level of aggression will have almost exactly the same distribution for experimental and control subjects. The unit of analysis is the *difference score*, the algebraic difference between the levels of aggression in the experiment between the two boys in each pair (e.g., experimental condition subject minus control condition subject). Thus the computation of t, based on difference scores, is essentially the same as that shown in Box 4.2 except that differences are between two matched individuals rather than the same individual at two different times. Typically, if the prior measure is positively correlated with the measure taken during the experiment, the matched pairs design will yield higher statistical power than the two independent random groups design.

Use of the t test is not confined to the experimental method. In addition to comparing two levels of a manipulated independent variable, two levels of a subject variable can also be compared with a t test. Consider the issue of whether boys and girls differ in levels of aggressive behavior in response to exposure to violent TV. Special care must be used in designing such a study. Samples must be selected so that the boys and girls are at least approximately the same on factors such as age and socioeconomic level. It would be desirable to select stimuli that are "gender neutral." That might be especially difficult in the present case where the actors depicting the violent behavior are more apt to be male than female. The aggression scores for boys and girls can be compared using the t test for independent groups (Box 4.1). The null hypothesis here is that the two mean values will be equal. Note the difference in interpretation of results here when testing this hypothesis and when testing the hypothesis of no effect of a manipulated independent variable. In the case of the independent variable manipulation, the researcher is apt to try to convince us that a statistically significant result supports the conclusion that changes in the dependent variable were caused by manipulation of the independent variable. In the case of a subject variable like gender, rejection of the null hypothesis cannot be used to imply causality, even for a well designed study. Any difference, or lack of difference for that matter, may be due to some unknown combination of biological and environmental factors that differentiate boys and girls.

4.3. Comparison of Two Samples With Nonparametric Tests

To illustrate another statistical test that may, under certain circumstances, be applied to the two independent random groups design, we describe a simple test called the *median test*. We illustrate this test with a case where the t test would usually be applied because the two independent random groups design and a continuous response measure are used. Suppose that the experimental group receives training with a particular memory aid, whereas the control group does not, and the number of errors on a recall test is recorded. Now suppose that the distribution of scores in the two groups is quite different—one is positively skewed (i.e., contains several extremely high outlier scores) and the other is negatively skewed (i.e., contains several extremely low outlier scores). Because the mean is the measure of average most sensitive to the presence of extreme scores, comparison of the number of errors made by the two groups may be distorted by the usual t test for the difference between two means. This extreme violation of the boundary conditions for using t leads to a different tactic. The specific test used is called the *median test*, because it classifies each score in terms of whether it is above or below the overall median for the two groups combined. Scores are then reduced to counts of the numbers above or below the overall median and these numbers are compared across groups, using χ^2. This is an example of a nonparametric test because it ignores the form of the distribution of numerical scores and abandons exact numerical values by merely recording whether each score is above or below some cutoff point. By reducing the amount of information retained, statistical power is reduced. Thus, despite its mathematical simplicity, this test should not be used unless the t test is manifestly inappropriate. Box 4.3 illustrates the median test.

Box 4.3. Application of the Median Test to Two Independent Random Groups Design

Independent variable manipulation: Subjects are randomly assigned to an experimental group that receives training with a memory aid and a control group that does not.

Dependent variable: The number of errors on a recall test is recorded for each subject. This would ordinarily lead to use of the t test for independent groups. However, assume the most severe form of departure from the normality assumption: Of the two distributions of scores, one is highly skewed in the positive direction and the other is highly skewed in the negative direction. Thus, the t test must be abandoned in favor of a nonparametric test, the "median" test.

Null hypothesis: When the scores for both groups are combined and an *overall* median is computed, half of the scores in *each* group will be above the overall median and half will be below it. H_0: $P_E = P_C = .5$, where P_E and P_C are the population values for the proportion of scores above the overall median in the experimental and control conditions, respectively.

Alternative hypothesis: If the researchers expect that there will be fewer errors in the experimental (memory aid) group, then H_a: $P_E < P_C$.

Compilation of data: After the scores for the two groups are combined to determine an overall median, each score in each group is coded as $+$ if it is above this value or $-$ if it is below this value. (Note that the exact numerical value of a score is no longer considered.) Scores that fall right on the overall median can be counted as one half $+$ and one half $-$.

	Condition	
	E	C
Above median ($+$)	10	15
Below median ($-$)	15	10

Calculation of χ^2: The expected value based on H_0 would be one half of 25 or 12.5 for each cell. Thus

$$\chi^2 = \frac{(10 - 12.5)^2}{12.5} + \frac{(15 - 12.5)^2}{12.5} + \frac{(15 - 12.5)^2}{12.5} + \frac{(10 - 12.5)^2}{12.5} = 2.00.$$

Decision: The calculated value is compared to the critical value in the χ^2 table (Appendix D). We use $df = 1$ because the data form a 2×2 table and $df =$ (number of rows $- 1$) $\times$ (number of columns $- 1$) or $(2 - 1)(2 - 1) = 1$. A one-tailed test is specified, so with $\alpha = .05$, we actually use the column labeled .10. The critical value we find is 2.71. Because the calculated value is less than the critical value, we must retain the null hypothesis that the groups are not different.

Another simple nonparametric test is available when order relations between two sets of scores can be determined even though exact numerical differences analyzed with t tests would be meaningless. The Mann–Whitney test is a more powerful test than χ^2 because it utilizes more information than whether or not a score exceeds some specified value. It applies to tests of hypotheses concerning ordinal data by taking into account the rank ordering of scores. An example given in Box 4.4 applies the Mann–Whitney test to the following hypothetical situation: A social scientist is interested in whether the evaluation of a president of the United States is higher for that generation of citizens who lived through his administration than for a later generation. The case in point is President John F. Kennedy. Persons from the Baby Boomer generation and Generation X are asked to rank President Kennedy in comparison to the presidents who came later. The Mann–Whitney test is used to compare the responses of the two groups.

Other nonparametric tests are available that focus on the rank ordering of scores. One such popular test is called the Wilcoxon rank sum test, which deals specifically with the matched pairs design and examines the rank ordering of the magnitude of signed difference scores (i.e., preserving the direction of difference) when scores within each pair are subtracted. The details of this test are given in several of the statistics texts referred to earlier.

4.4. Comparison of More Than Two Sample Means

4.4.1. One-Way Analysis of Variance

When there are only two levels of the independent variable in an independent random groups design, the t test and the F test in ANOVA are interchangeable. Calculations from the same data will yield a value of F that is equal to the square of the value of t (two-tailed case), but the "critical" value of F also is equal to the square of the "critical" value of t. Thus, the same decision will be reached regarding the hypotheses being tested. For more than two levels of the independent variable and a continuous dependent variable, one-way ANOVA is the procedure of choice.

Prototypical examples of the application of one-way ANOVA involve manipulation of an independent variable whose effects may vary as a function of its quantity, such as dosage of a drug, length of some treatment, amount of reinforcement, or size of a group. In

Box 4.4. Application of the Mann–Whitney U Test for Comparing Two Independent Groups

Subject variable: Subjects are selected from the Baby Boomer generation (born from 1945 to 1955) or from Generation X (born from 1970 to 1980).

Dependent variable: Each subject is asked to rank order the following presidents of the United States from best (1) to worst (8): Kennedy, Johnson, Nixon, Ford, Carter, Reagan, Bush, and Clinton.

Null hypothesis: The average rank for President Kennedy will be the same for the two populations.

Alternative hypothesis: The Baby Boomer generation will evaluate President Kennedy more favorably than will Generation X; that is, the average rank assigned to President Kennedy by the Baby Boomer generation will be higher than the average rank assigned by Generation X.

Compilation of data: To illustrate the calculations, we provide scores for a small sample of ten from each population, which we will identify as sample B (Baby Boomers) and sample X (Generation X). (In practice, we would use much larger samples.)

Scores for sample X: 7, 2, 4, 2, 6, 5, 1, 6, 3, 5

Scores for sample B: 6, 3, 5, 7, 1, 6, 4, 7, 2, 8

The scores are then rearranged and reassigned values in the following manner: First, the scores are combined across samples and arranged in order. For example, the top two scores are 1s, with one in each sample. These two scores each get the average rank of 1.5. The next three scores are 2s, representing ranks 3 through 5, so each gets the average rank of 4, and so forth. The sum of the ranks for all the scores in one sample is then computed, and the formula

$$U = N_1 N_2 + N_1 (N_1 + 1)/2 - T_1$$

is applied, where N_1 and N_2 are the two sample sizes and T_1 is the sum of the ranks for sample 1 (e.g., sample B). For these data, $N_1 = N_2 = 10$ and $T_1 = 93.5$. So,

$$U = 10 \times 10 + \frac{10 \times 11}{2} - 116.5 = 38.5.$$

The null hypothesis is tested by computing the statistic

$$\frac{U - E(U)}{\sigma}, \quad \text{where } E(U) = \frac{N_1 N_2}{2} = 50,$$

which represents the expected value of U if the two samples had identical ranks and

$$\sigma = \sqrt{\frac{N_1 N_2 (N_1 + N_2 + 1)}{12}} = 13.2, \quad \frac{U - E(U)}{\sigma} = \frac{38.5 - 50}{13.2} = -0.87.$$

This value is then compared to a critical value given in tables provided by Siegel (1956). In the present case, for $\alpha = .05$, the null hypothesis is retained.

other cases, different levels of the independent variable differ in qualitative ways such as when comparing several different treatments for depression.

One-way ANOVA can be applied to either a within-subject or a between-subjects experimental design using either complete randomization or matching. The measures of sampling error used as the denominator in the F test will differ across these different design characteristics; in general, this term will be lower for within-subject designs than for between-subjects designs, resulting in greater statistical power and higher values of F for within-subject designs.

Box 4.5 shows the application of one-way ANOVA to the case where patients suffering from depression are assigned to one of three dosages of an antidepressant drug. Following the initial F test, which showed a significant difference in depression across the three dosage levels, trend tests are performed that showed that depression decreases linearly with increased dosage. A graph of the results, likewise, would show a linear effect.

Although examining the effects of a numerical variable like drug dosage is a logical use of one-way ANOVA, so also are examinations of the effects of independent and subject variables whose levels are qualitatively different. Suppose, for example, that you were interested in comparing the effectiveness of several different therapeutic techniques for treating anxiety. You would use the same basic computational formulas as illustrated in Box 4.5, but, instead of following up a significant F test with a trend analysis, you would follow it up with specific comparisons between the various techniques. An example using a subject variable would be to use a single treatment and compare its effects on persons of different ethnic or racial backgrounds.

Some subject variables, however, are quantitative in nature. There is great interest, for example, in examining the aging process as it relates to various forms of behavior. Suppose you gave the same memory test to samples of subjects selected from the specific age categories 20, 40, 60, and 80. (A precaution here would be to use material to be recalled that is equally familiar to all groups.) One-way ANOVA could be used to compare the performance of the different age groups, and trend tests would provide a useful tool to look for linearity in the function relating memory to age. An alternative research design would be to select subjects of all ages, not just preselected categories, treat age as a continuous variable, and use correlation and regression for relating performance to age.

Box 4.5. Application of One-Way ANOVA to Independent Random Groups Design with More Than Two Levels

Independent variable manipulation: Patients suffering from depression are assigned at random to three different dosages of an antidepressant drug. Assume that the dosage levels are spaced equally apart; for example, 10, 15, and 20 units for levels 1, 2, and 3, respectively.

Dependent variable measure: Depression scores following treatment on a scale of 1 to 20. (An alternative is to measure depression before and after treatment, and use the change score as the dependent variable measure.)

Null hypothesis: The mean depression score is the same for each dosage. H_0: $\mu_1 = \mu_2 = \mu_3$, where μ_i is the population mean depression score for dosage i.

Alternative hypothesis: The mean depression score varies as a function of dosage.

Data compilation: The relevant summary data for each group are the sample size (n), the sum of the scores for all the subjects in the group (T), and the sum of the squared scores (ΣX^2). From these, the totals for all groups combined are also calculated.

Group	n	T	ΣX^2
1	20	170	1,470
2	20	130	870
3	20	100	540
	60	400	2,880

Using the computational formulas from Table 3.2, the following summary table was derived:

Source	df	SS	MS
Between groups	2	123	61.5
Within group	57	90	1.58
Total	59	213	

F test:

$$F = \frac{\text{MS between groups}}{\text{MS within group}} = \frac{61.5}{1.58} = 38.92.$$

Critical value: The table of critical values of F is given in Appendix C. For $\alpha = .05$ and $df = 2$ (numerator, shown by columns) and 57 (denominator, shown by rows, interpolating between $df = 40$ and 60), the critical value of F is 3.16.

Decision: Reject H_0 in favor of the alternative hypothesis that depression scores differ following treatment with different dosages.

Box 4.5. (*Continued*)

Trend analysis: To test whether the amount of depression decreases linearly across dosages, group totals are multiplied by the linear coefficients -1, 0, and 1. The resulting value, D, is squared and divided by n times the sum of the squared coefficients to yield SS linear:

$$D = (-1)(100) + (0)(130) + (1)(170) = 70,$$

$$\text{SS linear} = \frac{(70)^2}{20\left[(-1)^2 + (1)^2\right]} = 122.5 \quad \text{with } df = 1.$$

The linear component is tested for significance by dividing MS linear by MS within group:

$$F = \frac{122.5}{1.58} = 77.53 \quad \text{with } df = 1 \text{ and } 57.$$

The critical value for $\alpha = .05$ and these df is 4.01. Thus, we reject the null hypothesis of no linear trend. Note that SS linear was almost as large as SS between groups. As a consequence, "deviations from linearity" are nonsignificant, leading to the conclusion that depression decreases linearly with increases in dosage.

For the more general case where the levels of the variable are not equally spaced and a linear trend test is not appropriate, other tests are available for following up a significant F test to decide which particular means are different from each other. One such test, the Tukey test, involves calculating an "honestly significant difference" (HSD) from a formula that takes into account MS within group, the number of levels of the variable, sample sizes, and level of significance. If the absolute difference between any pair of means equals or exceeds HSD, then we reject the hypothesis of equality of these two means. In the present case, all three means are significantly different from each other.

4.4.2. Multifactor Analysis of Variance

Now suppose that a new antidepressant drug is to be tested and the researcher wants to study the effects of both the original drug, drug A, and the new drug, drug B, and, furthermore, wants to study them *in combination*. This calls for a factorial design where patients are given both drugs, in varying dosage combinations. If there are three dosages of each drug, there are nine unique combinations and nine different groups of patients are needed for the experiment. Of course, extensive pretesting is needed, perhaps with animals, to ensure that the strongest dosages, especially when combined, do not have harmful side effects. The question then is whether the antidepressant effect is greater when taking both drugs than when taking only one.

Box 4.6 shows the *two-way ANOVA* applied to this 3 × 3 factorial design. The fictitious data show that the higher the dosage of either drug, the greater the antidepressant effect. Furthermore, there is a significant interaction that shows that the effect of each drug depends on the level of the other drug taken with it.

The nature of the interaction can be illustrated best with a carefully constructed graph. Mean scores on the dependent variable, depression score following treatment, are plotted on the ordinate or *Y* axis. Levels of one independent variable, dosage of drug *A*, are plotted on the abscissa or *X* axis. Levels of the second independent variable, dosage of drug *B*, are plotted as separate lines on the graph. Parallel lines indicate a lack of interaction and additive effects of the two variables (i.e., the effect of increasing the dosage of one drug is the same, regardless of the dosage of the other drug). In Figure 4.1 the slopes of the lines show the effect of drug *A* dosage and differences between the elevation of the three lines show the effect of drug *B* dosage. The nonparallelism exhibited by the convergence of the lines in the lower right portion of the graph shows the interaction effect. The slope of each line indicates the magnitude of the effect of increasing dosages of drug *A* for subjects receiving a particular dosage of drug *B*. The line for the highest dosage of *B* is the flattest, indicating that the benefits of high dosage of one drug are reduced at high dosage of the other drug.

Calculations using multifactor ANOVA are the same regardless of whether the factors are manipulated independent variables or measured subject variables. In the drug example, both factors (dosages of *A* and *B*) are manipulated and subjects are assigned at random to combinations of *A* and *B*. Earlier, we said that even studies using the experimental method can benefit from inclusion of a subject variable. Drugs *A* and *B* might affect women and men differently. By formally including gender as a third factor, that is, by separately randomizing the assignment of women and men to the different dosage pairings, we would then have a 3 × 3 × 2 factorial design. The calculations are straightforward extensions of those shown in

Box 4.6. Application of Two-Way ANOVA to Factorial Design

Independent variable manipulations: Three dosages of drug A are used and three dosages of drug B. Subjects (patients suffering from depression) are assigned at random to the nine unique combinations of levels of A and levels of B. This defines a 3×3 factorial design and the appropriate statistical test is two-way ANOVA.

Dependent variable measure: Depression score following treatment.

Null hypotheses: There are three null hypotheses. The first says there is no effect of dosage of drug A. H_0: $\mu_{A1} = \mu_{A2} = \mu_{A3}$. The second says there is no effect of dosage of drug B. H_0: $\mu_{B1} = \mu_{B2} = \mu_{B3}$. The third says that the effect of varying dosage for drug A is the same at each dosage of drug B and vice versa. This is the hypothesis of no interaction.

Alternative hypotheses: For each null hypothesis there is a contrary alternative hypothesis: The mean depression score does vary as a function of dosage of drug A; the mean depression score varies as a function of dosage of drug B; changes in depression as a function of dosage of drug A differ at different dosages of drug B and vice versa.

Data compilation: The relevant summary data for each of the nine groups formed by all combinations of levels of drug A and levels of drug B are the sample size (n), the sum of the scores for that group (T), and the sum of the squared scores (ΣX^2).

	Dosage of Drug B		
	B1	B2	B3
A3	$n = 10$	$n - 10$	$n = 10$
	$T = 55$	$T = 50$	$T = 45$
	$\Sigma X^2 = 350$	$\Sigma X^2 = 275$	$\Sigma X^2 = 250$
A2	$n = 10$	$n = 10$	$n = 10$
	$T = 85$	$T = 58$	$T = 48$
	$\Sigma X^2 = 750$	$\Sigma X^2 = 350$	$\Sigma X^2 = 275$
A1	$n = 10$	$n = 10$	$n = 10$
	$T = 100$	$T = 75$	$T = 50$
	$\Sigma X^2 = 1050$	$\Sigma X^2 = 600$	$\Sigma X^2 = 300$

Using the computational formulas from Table 3.3, the following summary table was derived:

Source	df	SS	MS
Drug A	2	94.0	47.0
Drug B	2	158.4	79.2
Interaction	4	44.9	11.23
Within group	81	343.2	4.24
Total	89	640.5	

Box 4.6. (*Continued*)

F tests:
    Drug A: $F = 47.0/4.24 = 11.08$
    Drug B: $F = 79.2/4.24 = 18.68$
    Interaction: $F = 11.23/4.24 = 2.65$

Critical values: To test the effect of drug A and the effect of drug B, $df = 2$ and 81. To test the interaction, $df = 4$ and 81. From Appendix C, for $\alpha = .05$, the critical values are 3.11 and 2.49, respectively.

Decisions: Reject H_0 for drug A effects. Reject H_0 for drug B effects. Reject H_0 for the interaction. The key to understanding this pattern of results is to graph them. Figure 4.1 plots the mean depression score as a joint function of dosage of drug A and dosage of drug B. The general downward slope of the lines shows that scores decrease progressively over increasing dosages of drug A. The separation between the three lines reflects the fact that dosage of drug B also affected the scores. Perhaps the most interesting result is the convergence of the lines, indicating that the effect of increasing the dosage of each drug is the least when the other drug is at its highest dosage. There are diminishing returns for increasing the dosages of both drugs simultaneously.

Finally, following a two-way ANOVA, one may wish to compare the degree of influence or *proportion of variance accounted for* by each variable and their interaction. This is accomplished by simply taking each of the sum of squares (SS) terms and dividing by the total sum of squares. In the present case, these proportions are .14, .25, and .07, respectively, for drug A, drug B, and their interaction. Adding these values together, we can say that the systematic features of this experiment (varying dosages of drugs A and B) account for just under one half of the variance observed in the depression scores.

Table 3.3 and include the terms A, B, and gender main effects: interactions $A \times B$, $A \times$ gender, $B \times$ gender, and $A \times B \times$ gender.

Three-way interactions can be complex; for example, to be graphically illustrated, they typically require two panels rather than a single panel. However, they can reveal important aspects of the data. For example, suppose that combining high dosages of both drugs is beneficial to males, but detrimental to females (possibly due to biological differences). Then, the $A \times B$ interaction would be different for males and females, resulting in a significant three-way interaction, $A \times B \times$ gender. This is illustrated in Figure 4.2.

Adding the subject variable of gender has two possible advantages. First, if gender is a factor, then tests of the effects of drugs A and B and their interaction will have increased power by virtue of factoring

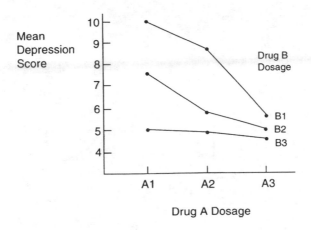

Figure 4.1. Graphic Representation of Two-Way Interaction

out gender. More importantly, the researcher can formally test whether the drugs affect women and men differently by examining the $A \times$ gender, $B \times$ gender, and $A \times B \times$ gender interactions.

These examples of multifactor ANOVA involve related independent variables; they were both manipulations of drug dosage. This need not be the case. In the area of consumer behavior, there is great interest in how consumers make trade-offs between cost and quality factors. In a typical application of a factorial design, subjects would be asked to rate their opinion of each of a series of products of a given class (e.g., television sets) that vary in both price and length of warranty. Two-way ANOVA would then be used to decompose these purchase likelihood judgments into the effect of price, the effect of length of warranty, and the interaction between the two. A marketing researcher might be particularly interested in the relative size of the effects of price and warranty (as indicated by the sum of squares terms), so that future product designs could be sensitive to consumer values.

4.5. Comparisons Involving Frequency or "Count" Data

The χ^2 test is used for frequency or count data when each subject's response falls into one and only one of a discrete number of

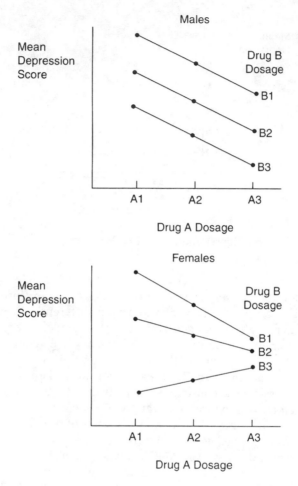

Figure 4.2. Graphic Representation of Three-Way Interaction

mutually exclusive and exhaustive categories. These tests can be used in a study involving a single factor or multiple factors. We consider each case in turn.

Suppose that a leading soft drink manufacturer has developed a new diet cola and wants to compare perceptions of taste between the new brand and the three leading brands of diet cola. Each participant in a taste test samples each brand in an unmarked cup and selects the best tasting one. A counterbalanced order of presentation is used such that across participants each brand appears equally often in the first, second, third, and fourth positions. As an example of this form of counterbalancing, subjects are assigned at random to one of the following four sequences for sampling brands *A* through *D*: *ABCD*, *BCDA*, *CDAB*, and *DABC*. (This makes it an example of the experimental method.) Sufficient time is given between successive tastes to eliminate the effects of aftertaste.

The primary data are the number of times each brand is selected as the best tasting. There are several ways to use χ^2 here and several ways to act on the results. The first way is to test the null hypothesis that all four colas are chosen an equal proportion of the time. The second way is to focus on the new brand and compare its frequency of choice with the average of the other three brands. A third way is to compare the new brand with each of the other brands, in turn. The first of these tests involves 3 degrees of freedom because there are four categories to be compared. The remaining tests involve 1 degree of freedom because there are two categories to be compared. These tests are illustrated in Box 4.7.

χ^2 can also be used as a *test of contingency* between two categorical variables. Suppose that a political organization wants to know if their two leading candidates have differential appeal to men and women voters. Representative samples of male and female voters would be asked over the telephone which candidate they prefer. Each observation falls into one and only one cell of the table representing the combination of voter gender and preferred candidate. This table, known as the "contingency table," will be illustrated in Box 4.8. (Because this study involves no manipulation of variables or random assignment of subjects to different conditions, this is an example of the method of observation rather than the experimental method.) Primary data would be the proportion of male and proportion of female respondents favoring each candidate. A significant χ^2 would mean that these proportions differ and that support for a candidate was thus contingent on the gender of the voter. Follow-up tests could be conducted for each gender separately to see if there was significant preference for one candidate over the other within each gender. These tests are shown in Box 4.8.

Another useful application of χ^2 is determining whether an empirical distribution of scores fits a particular form. Suppose you are interested in determining whether a particular trait or characteristic

---

Box 4.7. Application of χ^2 for a Single Categorical Variable

Independent variable manipulation: Each of a sample of consumers is given four different brands of diet cola to taste. The brands are presented in a counterbalanced order.

Dependent variable measure: Which brand is selected as the best tasting.

Null hypothesis: The proportion of individuals in the population selecting each brand will be the same. H_0: $P_A = P_B = P_C = P_D$, where P_i is the proportion of the population choosing brand i.

Alternative hypothesis: The proportion selecting each brand will not be the same. (In particular, the investigator wants to see if there is a preference for the new brand, brand A.)

Data compilation: The number of persons in the sample who select each brand.

Brand A	Brand B	Brand C	Brand D
27	21	22	30

Calculation of χ^2: If the null hypothesis were true, the expected frequencies would be 25 for each brand. Using the formula for χ^2 given earlier,

$$\chi^2 = \frac{(27-25)^2}{25} + \frac{(21-25)^2}{25} + \frac{(22-25)^2}{25} + \frac{(30-25)^2}{25} = 2.16.$$

Critical value: The table of critical values of χ^2 is given in Appendix D. For $\alpha = .05$ (fourth column) and $df = 3$ (third row), the critical value of χ^2 is 7.82.

Decision: Retain H_0. There is insufficient evidence that one cola is preferred over the others. The same conclusion would apply if cola A were compared to the average of the others or if A were compared to each of the others.

---

is normally distributed within a target population. Let us say that you are looking at depression among students at your college or university. You administer a standard scale of depression (i.e., one whose reliability and validity have been established in prior research) to a random sample of 250 students. You compute the mean and standard deviation of these 250 scores. Of course, one of the things you would want to do is to compare your mean with published means from other populations. You then determine what percentages of your scores fall into specific intervals within the distribution: between the

Box 4.8. Application of χ^2 for Test of Contingency Between Two Categorical Variables

Independent variable manipulation: Present voters with a choice between two leading political candidates.

Subject variable: Gender of voter.

Dependent variable measure: Which candidate is preferred.

Null hypothesis: There will be no contingency between the gender of voter and the choice of candidate. That is, the proportion of voters choosing candidate A over candidate B will be the same for female and male voters. H_0: $P_{A,F} = P_{A,M}$ and $P_{B,F} = P_{B,M}$. (Note the use of proportions rather than frequences in H_0. This is because there need be no restriction that there are equal numbers of males, M, and females, F, in the sample. Thus the hypotheses are stated in terms of the proportion of voters of each gender choosing each candidate.)

Alternative hypothesis: Degree of preference for one candidate over another will depend on voter gender. H_a: $P_{A,F} \neq P_{A,M}$ and $P_{B,F} \neq P_{B,M}$.

Compilation of data: The number of voters in the sample selecting each candidate will be counted separately for males and females.

Candidate	Voter Gender		
Selected	Female	Male	Total
A	25	20	45
B	15	40	55
	40	60	

Of the 40 female voters, 25 chose A and 15 chose B; of the 60 male voters, 20 chose A and 40 chose B.

Calculation of χ^2: Overall, 45 of the voters chose A and 55 chose B. Expected values based on H_0 are that the 45%:55% split holds for both female and male voters; that is,

Candidate		
Selected	Female	Male
A	45% of 40 = 18	45% of 60 = 27
B	55% of 40 = 22	55% of 60 = 33

Comparing these expected values with the observed values, we obtain

$$\chi^2 = \frac{(25-18)^2}{18} + \frac{(20-27)^2}{27} + \frac{(15-22)^2}{22} + \frac{(40-33)^2}{33} = 8.24.$$

60

Box 4.8. (*Continued*)

Critical value: In a contingency table, *df* equals the number of rows minus 1 times the number of columns minus 1, or $(2 - 1)(2 - 1) = 1$. For $\alpha = .05$ and $df = 1$, the critical value of χ^2 is 3.84.

Decision: Reject H_0 in favor of the alternative that the relative preference for A over B is greater for females than for males, and conversely for preference of B over A.

Follow-up tests: To separately examine each gender's choices, we consider each column of the table separately and compare the observed numbers with a 50:50 split:

for female voters,

$$\chi^2 = \frac{(25 - 20)^2}{20} + \frac{(15 - 20)^2}{20} = 2.50;$$

for male voters,

$$\chi^2 = \frac{(20 - 30)^2}{30} + \frac{(40 - 30)^2}{30} = 6.67.$$

With $\alpha = .05$ and $df = 1$, the value for males is statistically significant, but the value for females is not. Thus, we reject the null hypothesis for males, but not for females. We conclude that male voters prefer candidate B over candidate A, but that there is not a clear preference among females.

---

mean and 1 standard deviation above the mean, between the mean and 1 standard deviation below the mean, between 1 and 2 standard deviations above the mean, between 1 and 2 standard deviations below the mean, more than 2 standard deviations above the mean, and more than 2 standard deviations below the mean.

Within a normal distribution, these percentages would be 34, 34, 13.5, 13.5, 2.5, and 2.5, respectively, which correspond to frequencies of 85, 85, 34, 34, 6, and 6 for a sample of size 250. You can then compare observed and expected frequencies in these different intervals using χ^2. Suppose that the observed frequencies were 80, 85, 40,

25, 15, and 5, respectively. Then

$$\chi^2 = \frac{(80 - 85)^2}{85} + \frac{(85 - 85)^2}{85} + \frac{(40 - 34)^2}{34} + \frac{(25 - 34)^2}{34}$$

$$+ \frac{(15 - 6)^2}{6} + \frac{(5 - 6)^2}{6} = 17.41.$$

With 5 degrees of freedom (there were six categories) and using $\alpha = .05$, this is a significant value. A nonsignificant χ^2 would have meant that the scores do not deviate significantly from a normal distribution. A significant χ^2 means that you have a nonnormal distribution, which might lead you to look for factors that skewed the distribution of depression scores at your institution (the main contributor to the significant χ^2 in this case is the disproportionately large number of students more than 2 standard deviations above the mean); for example, factors that might increase depression within a particular subgroup.

4.6. Analyzing Relationships Between Naturally Occurring Variables

4.6.1. Correlation

The correlation coefficient is often used to quantify the degree of relationship observed between two naturally occurring variables. For example, a recent newspaper report cited a study linking country music and suicide. For each of a number of cities, the suicide rate (number of suicides per 10,000 population) was recorded as well as the radio audience share listening to local country music stations. Using calculations like those illustrated in Box 4.9, the researchers obtained a significant positive correlation between these two measures.

The mass media report could not avoid the temptation of concluding that the sad lyrics of contemporary country music caused some individuals with a predisposition toward suicide to commit the act. Such a causal interpretation of a correlation is, of course, premature. The opposite direction of causality cannot be ruled out; persons on the verge of suicide may be attracted to sad songs. Any of a number of third factors may be involved in the causal link: sociodemographic,

---

Box 4.9. Application of Correlation Coefficient to Observed Relation Between Two Variables

Measures: For each city in the sample, the suicide rate (Y) was recorded and the market share of the local country music stations (X).

Null hypothesis: There is no relationship between the two variables. H_0: $\rho_{XY} = 0$, where ρ_{XY} is the correlation between X and Y for the population of cities from which the sample was selected.

Alternative hypothesis: There is a positive relationship between the two variables. H_a: $\rho_{XY} > 0$.

Compilation of data: For each city, the values needed to compute r, the sample correlation, are X, Y, XY, X^2, and Y^2. For example, city 1 might have $X = 13$, $Y = 6$, $XY = 78$, $X^2 = 169$, and $Y^2 = 36$. The sum of each of these values across cities constitutes the terms used in the computational version of the formula for r.

Computation of r: The computational formula for r is

$$r = \frac{\Sigma\, XY - (\Sigma\, X)(\Sigma\, Y)/n}{\sqrt{\left[\Sigma\, X^2 - (\Sigma\, X)^2/n\right]\left[\Sigma\, Y^2 - (\Sigma\, Y)^2/n\right]}}.$$

This formula is mathematically equivalent to the definitional formula given in the text. Say, for a sample of 30 cities, $\Sigma\, X = 400$, $\Sigma\, Y = 180$, $\Sigma\, XY = 3450$, $\Sigma\, X^2 = 7{,}500$, and $\Sigma\, Y^2 = 3{,}500$. Then $r = .46$.

Test of significance of r: To test the hypothesis that the population correlation is zero, the following t test is used:

$$t = r\sqrt{\frac{n-2}{1-r^2}} \quad \text{(with } df = n - 2\text{)}$$

$$= 2.74.$$

For $\alpha = .05$ with a one-tailed test and $df = 28$, the critical value of t is 1.70. This illustrates a use of the t test beyond the usual comparison of two mean values.

Decision: Reject H_0 in favor of the alternative hypothesis that country music radio share and suicide rate are positively correlated. Recall, however, that such a result says nothing about the direction of causality.

---

economic, and geographic factors may differentiate cities varying in both suicide rate and country music popularity. For example, people in a particular occupation may be especially high in both suicide rate and preference for country music, and this occupation may be more common in some cities than in others. Uncovering such a relationship is provocative and may foster future, more revealing research.

Perhaps a more common application of the correlation coefficient among social scientists is to look for links between personal characteristics; that is, two characteristics that describe the same individual. Let us say that we want to determine the strength of relationship between a person's income (X) and the amount they give to charity each year (Y). Using pairs of scores for these two quantities will undoubtedly lead to a substantial and statistically significant value of r, because the rich can afford to give more. A more interesting question is how large r would be if the pairs of scores for each individual were defined as X equals annual income and Y equals percentage of annual income given to charity. This might be an even fairer assessment of whether people give "their fair share."

A final, innovative use of the correlation coefficient by social scientists involves correlating two personal characteristics over some period of time using what is called *time-lag* or *longitudinal methods*. It is well known that the extent of exposure to violence in the mass media correlates with amount of aggressive behavior in children. Like all such correlations, it is difficult to assess the direction of causality of this relationship. A group of researchers (Lefkowitz, Eron, Walder, and Huesmann, 1977) followed a group of children over a 10-year period, measuring preference for violent TV and amount of aggression at age 8, and then, for the same individuals, measuring these same quantities at age 18. Of special interest was the correlation between TV violence at age 8 and aggression at age 18 compared to the correlation between aggression at age 8 and TV violence at age 18. As seen in Figure 4.3, only the first of these correlations was significantly greater than zero. This led the researchers to conclude that the most plausible causal hypothesis is that a preference for watching violent television at age 8 contributes to the development of aggressive habits that persist at least to age 18. They reasoned that if the causal link were in the opposite direction, then violent tendencies at age 8 would have been predictive of TV preferences at age 18, which they were not. That is, differences in TV viewing behavior at age 8 were predictive of aggression at age 18, but

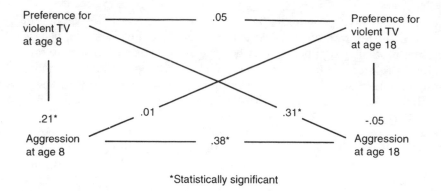

*Statistically significant

Figure 4.3. Correlations in a Time-Lag Study [Data from M. M. Lefkowitz, L. D. Eron, L. O. Walder, and L. R. Huesmann (1977), *Growing Up to Be Violent*, Pergamon Press, Elmsford, New York.]

differences in aggression at age 8 were not predictive of TV viewing behavior at age 18, and this asymmetry led to the researchers' conclusion about causality.

4.6.2. Multiple Regression

Multiple regression can be used to assess how much of the variance in a particular measure can be accounted for by a given set of factors. Alternatively, it can be used to predict the value of some future measure (the criterion variable) from a set of prior indicators (predictor variables). Let us consider the case where we want to predict a student's undergraduate performance at some college or university based on that student's prior record. Why would we want to do this? This would be useful to a counselor advising students as to whether they should try a certain college in the first place or whether they should select a relatively lax curriculum or a demanding curriculum like an honors program.

We start by examining the records of the students over some particular period of time. For each student, we have a record of their college grade point average as well as their background. The criterion variable is college grade point average and the predictor variables include high school grade point average, difficulty of high school curriculum, and college entrance exam scores. As shown in Box 4.10, a regression equation would be derived based on the

Box 4.10. Application of Multiple Regression

Criterion variable: The score that the investigators want to predict is grade point average at a particular college. The higher the degree of relationship between this criterion variable and the predictor variables, as evidenced by data from past students, the more accurate will be the prediction for a new student.

Predictor variables: High school grade point average (GPA on a scale of 0 to 4), difficulty of high school curriculum (number of math and science courses taken), and college entrance exam scores (e.g., compositive standard score).

Null hypotheses: The multiple correlation coefficient, R, that relates predicted values of the criterion variable to obtained values will be zero. Additional hypotheses concern the incremental contribution of each individual predictor variable, after the effects of the other variables are removed. Tests of these additional hypotheses require calculation of "partial correlations," which will not be covered here. The interested reader is referred to Hays (1994).

Alternative hypotheses: The multiple correlation will be greater than zero. The individual partial correlations will be different from zero. (For the predictor variables listed here, the expectations would be for partial correlations greater than zero. In other cases, negative partial correlations would also be informative and contribute to predictions, such as the influence of number of hours employed in a job on college grade point average.)

Compilation of data: For each of a sample of past students who have graduated from this college, say $n = 200$, their overall grade point average would be recorded, as well as their college entrance exam scores and their relevant high school performance measures.

Here's a hypothetical example using the variables listed here:

Multiple $R = .80$, $R^2 = .64$

Predictor Variable	b	t
High school GPA	.80	4.85
No. math courses	.25	2.50
No. science courses	.10	1.11
College entrance exam	1.23	6.02

Decisions: Each coefficient, b, reflects the number of units that the criterion variable is predicted to change given a one-unit change in that predictor variable, holding all other predictor variables constant. The t test for each predictor variable equals the value of the regression coefficient, b, divided by its standard error, which is a measure of how the influence of that factor varies over students. Degrees of freedom equal $n - 1$. In the foregoing example, all values of t are significant except for number of science courses taken in high school. Furthermore, the multiple correlation coefficient R is also significantly different from zero. $R^2 = .64$ means that 64% of the variance in college GPA can be accounted for or explained by this set of predictors. Thus, all null hypotheses are rejected except for the one concerning number of science courses.

Box 4.10. (*Continued*)

Predictions: For new students, college GPA (*Y*) can be predicted from the students'
high school GPAs (X_1), the number of math courses they have taken (X_2), the
number of science courses they have taken (X_3), and their college entrance exam
composite scores (X_4). Suppose that a new student's high school GPA was 3.50,
she had six semesters of math and four semesters of science in high school, and
her standardized college entrance exam score was 1.5 (i.e., 1.5 standard deviation
units above the national mean). In addition, a constant term is added (*a* in the
regression equation) to represent the intercept of the regression line. In this case,
the constant is -3.25. Then

$$Y = -3.25 + .80 \times 3.50 + .25 \times 6 + .10 \times 4 + 1.23 \times 1.5 = 3.30.$$

So, we would predict that this student will do well in her new college.

---

relationship between predictor variable scores and criterion variable
scores for past students at that college. For a new student, that
student's scores on the predictor variables would be plugged into the
equation and a value would be estimated for the criterion. Of course,
this estimate would not be precise; any given student's motivation
and work habits could change considerably from high school to
college. However, to the extent that the selected predictor variables
provide accurate estimates, as indicated by the value of R^2 in the
regression analysis, this method can represent a big improvement
over an estimate not based on the empirical relations used in
regression analysis.

As another example, clinical psychologists and personality theorists
have developed a "big 5" inventory of individual difference factors
that contribute to a person's mental health or emotional well-being
(John, Donahue, and Kentle, 1991). These individual difference factors are assessed from a survey consisting of the following subscales:
openness to experience, conscientiousness, extroversion, agreeable-
ness, and neuroticism. The research issue is how well these factors
predict overall mental health and well-being. To apply multiple
regression analysis to this issue, each individual in the study would be
administered the survey, where scores on the five subscales constitute
the predictor variables. The criterion variable(s) would be assess-
ments of overall well-being or mental health based on self-reports,

peer ratings, or ratings by clinicians. The statistical output would indicate which of the five predictors contributed significantly to the criterion measures above and beyond the contributions of the other predictors, and, perhaps more importantly, the overall predictive accuracy (R^2) of the complete "big 5" inventory.

Multiple regression can be used not only to understand the factors or values that relate to an individual's behavior, but also to understand values that apply to the larger society. Take the case of sentences for convicted criminals. Using criminal trial records for the data, analyses could be performed with the length of prison sentence for convicted criminals serving as the criterion variable. Predictor variables would include personal characteristics of the criminal such as race, gender, age, and other socioeconomic indicators. Personal characteristics of the victim of the crime could also be included as predictor variables, as well as the relationship of perpetrator to victim. The type or severity of the crime could be included as an additional predictor variable; alternatively, separate analyses could be done for each type of crime. A possible provocative outcome would be that, beyond the influence of all other variables, crimes committed against whites by nonwhites are penalized the most.

Table 4.1 summarizes the material in this section by giving, for each of the major statistical tests, the guidelines for its application and a prototypical example of an experiment to which that test should be applied. The reader should then use these guidelines and prototypes to determine where a new application best fits.

68

TABLE 4.1
Summary Table

Stat. Test	Resp. Measures	Typical H_0	Other Assumptions	Example
χ^2	Counts, frequency data	$P_1 = P_2$ (proportions)	Independent observations that fall into mutually exclusive and exhaustive categories	Do more males than females believe in capital punishment?
Mann–Whitney (and other nonparametric tests)	Rank orders	Two population distributions are equal	Underlying variable is continuously distributed	How do two generations differ in ranking a historical figure?
t (independent groups)	Continuous (interval or ratio scales)	$\mu_E = \mu_C$ (means)	Normal distributions, equal variances	Does amount of aggression differ for children exposed to violent and nonviolent TV?
t (difference scores)	Continuous (interval or ratio scales)	$\mu_D = 0$	Difference scores normally distributed	Are scores on a depression index reduced after treatment?
One-way ANOVA (F test)	Continuous (interval or ratio scales)	$\mu_1 = \mu_2 = \mu_3$	Normal distributions, equal variances	How does length/dosage of treatment affect reduction in symptoms?
Multifactor ANOVA (F tests)	Continuous (interval or ratio scales)	1. $\mu_{R1} = \mu_{R2}$ 2. $\mu_{C1} = \mu_{C2}$ 3. $\mu_{R1C1} - \mu_{R1C2} = \mu_{R2C1} - \mu_{R2C2}$ (no interaction)	Normal distributions, equal variances	Does amount of drinking in college students depend on gender and whether or not the student belongs to a fraternity or sorority?
Correlation (Pearson r)	Paired continuous observations	$\rho = 0$	Linear relationship between the two variables	What is the relationship between hours of employment and grade point average?
Multiple regression	Triads, etc., of continuous or categorical variables	$b_1 = 0$ $b_2 = 0$ $b_3 = 0$	Linear relationships between the predictor variables and the criterion variable	How does the likelihood of getting into graduate school depend on your grade point average, scores on standardized tests, amount of research experience, and content of letters of recommendation?

5. CONCLUSION

Let us summarize the main points made in this monograph. First and foremost, this monograph is meant to provide a wedding of the principles of good research design and appropriate use of statistical tests. Statistical hypothesis testing can be an important tool for the social scientist because these tests provide objective rules for deciding when relationships uncovered in sample data are likely to represent more than chance fluctuations. The logic behind the tests is one of "indirect support"; the hypothesis of an experimental effect is supported when the hypothesis of no effect or null hypothesis is rejected. We start by assuming the null hypothesis to be true; then we calculate the probability of obtaining a value equal to or more extreme than the test statistic, under the assumption that the null hypothesis is true. We reject the null hypothesis when this probability turns out to be less than a predetermined value, called the level of significance. In any one instance, this objective decision can be wrong; that would be a Type I error in the case of mistakenly rejecting the null hypothesis or a Type II error in the case of mistakenly retaining the null hypothesis. At least we know that the computational process by which we arrived at the decision was unbiased and, in the long run, not apt to lead to inflated claims.

One of the main points of this monograph, however, is that research conclusions based on computed statistical values are valid only insofar as the data used to calculate these values were collected in an appropriate manner. A variety of research designs is available to the social scientist seeking to establish, interpret, and apply relationships between the factors of interest. Initial decisions center around the issue of causality. Is the goal to determine the direction of causality between the variables that enter into a relationship or to determine the existence of a relationship that permits predictions of future events? Either way, potential sources of bias need to be identified and brought under control. Specific experimental design features were discussed that deal with biased behavior, biased scoring, and biased assignment of subjects to experimental conditions.

The researcher must weigh the pros and cons of a particular technique as they apply to the specific research problem. For example, choice of a within-subject versus between-subjects design may depend on whether the particular type of carryover effect likely to occur in the task can be equated across conditions through a simple counterbalancing procedure. The wisdom of relying on simple randomization as opposed to more complicated techniques to control subject variables depends on sample size, population homogeneity, and whether there is a readily identifiable "matching" variable that is correlated with the behavior under investigation.

To assure that the data obtained from a study can be analyzed and interpreted in a proper manner, choice of the appropriate statistical test should be an integral part of the design of the study. The present contention is that this is one of the most important, but least emphasized, parts of research design.

We presented guidelines for the application of the different statistical tests. The type of response measure was an important consideration. χ^2 tests are used with frequency or count data as long as each subject's response can fall into only one of the several mutually exclusive categories. In addition, χ^2 can be used to test the contingency between two categorical variables. Nonparametric tests such as Mann–Whitney are used to test hypotheses about ordered data. Hypotheses concerning arithmetic response measures, such as comparisons of mean response times or mean numbers of errors or mean ratings, are tested with t or F as long as the assumptions of normality and homogeneity of variance are not seriously violated.

Choice of specific t tests or F tests depends on characteristics of the experimental design. Hypotheses concerning two independent random groups designs with continuous response measures are evaluated with the t test for independent groups, which requires computation of the mean and standard deviation for each of the two samples. The null hypothesis is that the populations from which the two samples were drawn have equal means. The prototypical experimental group–control group design provides an example. When the independent random groups design is extended to more than two levels of the independent variable, such as comparing several dosages of a drug, then the F test is used in a one-way ANOVA.

When the two levels of the independent variable are administered to the same subject at different times or are administered to two different subjects who are "matched" on some relevant subject variable, then a different version of the t test is employed. The unit of analysis is the difference score, and calculations include the mean and standard deviation of the sample of difference scores. The null hypothesis is that the population of difference scores has a mean of zero. The prototypical before–after design relies on this test.

When two or more factors are combined in a design that includes all possible combinations of factor levels, this is called a factorial design, and, for continuous response measures, the multifactor ANOVA is used to test the hypotheses of interest. These hypotheses include the separate effect of each variable, unconfounded by levels of the other variables, and the interactions between variables. The null hypothesis for interaction between two variables is that the effect of one variable is the same across levels of the other variable. This translates into the parallelism test for a graphic display of the results. Some interesting applications of such tests occur when one factor is a manipulated independent variable and the other factor is a measured subject variable, such as testing whether the comparative effectiveness of different drugs or therapies differs for males and females.

The correlation coefficient is used to quantify the relationship between paired observations such as length of time in treatment and recovery from depression. When there are several variables related to and predictive of some criterion measure, then multiple regression is used to make predictions and assess the reliability of these predictions. Predicting future economic trends based on a variety of indexes of past economic performance is a practical example.

Figure 5.1 summarizes much of the discussion in this section through a simple flow diagram for the decision of which statistical

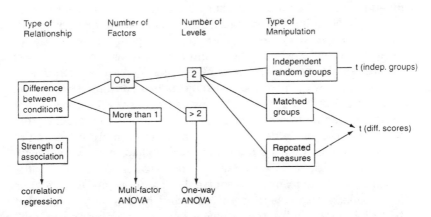

Figure 5.1. Flow Diagram for Selecting the Appropriate Statistical Test with Continuous (Interval or Ratio) Response Scales

test to select. The choice points depicted in Figure 5.1 are for continuous response scales that have ratio or interval properties, or at least approximate these properties, and depend on whether hypotheses deal with the difference between conditions or the strength of association, whether there is more than one factor (independent variable and/or subject variable) in the experimental design, the number of levels of the factor if there is a single factor, and whether the single factor varies between subjects or within subjects. Of course, when response scales have only nominal or ordinal properties, nonparametric tests such as χ^2 or Mann–Whitney are used.

Now let us return to the example of the students who studied college drinking behavior. First, let us briefly discuss their choice of research method. They chose the observational method using a survey instrument rather than the experimental method, because it would be impractical and unethical to try to manipulate drinking behavior. Additionally, of course, they could not have assigned subjects at random to join or not join Greek fraternal organizations. Their methodology relied on self-reports, which could be seen as a drawback, but respondents were assured of anonymity, so there was no obvious reason to falsify responses.

Because the student–researchers asked a variety of questions in their survey, including questions with both continuous and dichotomous scales, they used several different statistical tests. Subjects were asked whether they engaged in binge drinking (after that term was defined to them). For binge drinkers, a 2×2 χ^2 test of contingency was conducted using the categories of gender and whether or not they belonged to a Greek organization. A significant value of χ^2 indicated that males who binge are more likely to be Greek members than are females who binge. A parallel question using a continuous measure was how many drinks the subjects had consumed during the past two weeks. Two-way ANOVA was used here, with a significant interaction leading to much the same conclusion as that arising from the χ^2 test of contingency. Fraternity men drank more often and in greater quantities than nonfraternity men and women. (Generalization of these results to universities other than the one where the study was conducted would, of course, be inappropriate.)

The student–researchers were interested in determining to what extent differences in drinking behavior between members of a Greek organization and non-Greeks were due to the possibility that students who opt to join fraternities or sororities were more apt to be drinkers in high school. Another two-way ANOVA with self-reported drinking amounts in high school as the dependent variable verified that fraternity members reported disproportionately high amounts of drinking in high school. Finally, a multiple regression was conducted with number of drinks during the past two weeks as the criterion variable, and gender, membership in a Greek organization, and self-reported drinking amounts in high school as the predictor variables. All these predictor variables were significant. The conclusion is that the greater drinking exhibited by fraternity members can be accounted for by a combination of the following factors: (1) men drank more than women; (2) fraternity members were more apt to be drinkers before college; and (3) membership in a fraternity increased the use of alcohol.

The use of χ^2, ANOVA, and regression in the same study is the exception rather than the rule. This example, however, illustrates quite nicely how the selection of statistical test depends on the particular questions being asked and how these questions are operationalized in the design of the study. The intent here was to provide sufficient guidelines and examples to make it easier for researchers and students to make the right choices for the right reasons.

APPENDIX A: RANDOM NUMBERS

	Column Number							
Row	00000 01234	00000 56789	11111 01234	11111 56789	22222 01234	22222 56789	33333 01234	33333 56789
				Fifth Thousand				
00	29935	06971	63175	52579	10478	89379	61428	21363
01	15114	07126	51890	77787	75510	13103	42942	48111
02	03870	43225	10589	87629	22039	94124	38127	65022
03	79390	39188	40756	45269	65959	20640	14284	22960
04	30035	06915	79196	54428	64819	52314	48721	81594
05	29039	99861	28759	79802	68531	39198	38137	24373
06	78196	08108	24107	49777	09599	43569	84820	94956
07	15847	85493	91442	91351	80130	73752	21539	10986
08	36614	62248	49194	97209	92587	92053	41021	80064
09	40549	54884	91465	43862	35541	44466	88894	74180
10	40878	08997	14286	09982	90308	78007	51587	16658
11	10229	49282	41173	31468	59455	18756	08908	06660
12	15918	76787	30624	25928	44124	25088	31137	71614
13	13403	18796	49909	94404	64979	41462	18155	98335
14	66523	94596	74908	90271	10009	98648	17640	68909
15	91665	36469	68343	17870	25975	04662	21272	50620
16	67415	87515	08207	73729	73201	57593	96917	69699
17	76527	96996	23724	33448	63392	32394	60887	90617
18	19815	47789	74348	17147	10954	34355	81194	54407
19	25592	53587	76384	72575	84347	68918	05739	57222
20	55902	45539	63646	31609	95999	82887	40666	66692
21	02470	58376	79794	22482	42423	96162	47491	17264
22	18630	53263	13319	97619	35859	12350	14632	87659
23	89673	38230	16063	92007	59503	38402	76450	33333
24	62986	67364	06595	17427	84623	14565	82860	57300

Taken from M. G. Kendall and B. B. Smith (1938), Randomness and random sampling numbers, *Journal of the Royal Statistical Society*, *101*, 147–166, by permission of the Royal Statistical Society.

APPENDIX B: DISTRIBUTION OF t

One-tailed: Two-tailed: n	$P = .05$ $P = .1$	.025 .05	.01 .02	.005 .01	.0005 .001
1	6.314	12.706	31.821	63.657	636.619
2	2.920	4.303	6.965	9.925	31.598
3	2.353	3.182	4.541	5.841	12.941
4	2.132	2.776	3.747	4.604	8.610
5	2.015	2.571	3.365	4.032	6.859
6	1.943	2.447	3.143	3.707	5.959
7	1.895	2.365	2.998	3.499	5.405
8	1.860	2.306	2.896	3.355	5.041
9	1.833	2.262	2.821	3.250	4.781
10	1.812	2.228	2.764	3.169	4.587
11	1.796	2.201	2.718	3.106	4.437
12	1.782	2.179	2.681	3.055	4.318
13	1.771	2.160	2.650	3.012	4.221
14	1.761	2.145	2.624	2.977	4.140
15	1.753	2.131	2.602	2.947	4.073
16	1.746	2.120	2.583	2.921	4.015
17	1.740	2.110	2.567	2.898	3.965
18	1.734	2.101	2.552	2.878	3.922
19	1.729	2.093	2.539	2.861	3.883
20	1.725	2.086	2.528	2.845	3.850
21	1.721	2.080	2.518	2.831	3.819
22	1.717	2.074	2.508	2.819	3.792
23	1.714	2.069	2.500	2.807	3.767
24	1.711	2.064	2.492	2.797	3.745
25	1.708	2.060	2.485	2.787	3.725
26	1.706	2.056	2.479	2.779	3.707
27	1.703	2.052	2.473	2.771	3.690
28	1.701	2.048	2.467	2.763	3.674
29	1.699	2.045	2.462	2.756	3.659
30	1.697	2.042	2.457	2.750	3.646
40	1.684	2.021	2.423	2.704	3.551
60	1.671	2.000	2.390	2.660	3.460
120	1.658	1.980	2.358	2.617	3.373
∞	1.645	1.960	2.326	2.576	3.291

Adapted from Table IV of Fisher (1942), *Statistical Methods for Research Workers*, 3rd ed., Oliver and Boyd, Ltd., Edinburgh, by permission of the publishers.

APPENDIX C: UPPER PERCENTAGE POINTS
OF *F* DISTRIBUTION

df denom- inator	df Numerator									
	1	2	3	4	5	6	7	8	9	10
	$\alpha = .05$									
1	161.4	199.5	215.8	224.8	230.0	233.8	236.5	238.6	240.1	242.1
2	18.51	19.00	19.16	19.25	19.30	19.33	19.35	19.37	19.38	19.40
3	10.13	9.55	9.28	9.12	9.01	6.94	6.89	6.85	6.81	6.79
4	7.71	6.94	6.59	6.39	6.26	6.16	6.09	6.04	6.00	5.96
5	6.61	5.79	5.41	5.19	5.05	4.95	4.88	4.82	4.77	4.74
6	5.99	5.14	4.75	4.53	4.39	4.28	4.21	4.15	4.10	4.05
7	5.59	4.74	4.35	4.12	3.97	3.82	3.79	3.73	3.68	3.64
8	5.32	4.46	4.07	3.84	3.69	3.58	3.50	3.44	3.39	3.35
9	5.12	4.26	3.65	3.63	3.48	3.37	3.29	3.23	3.18	3.14
10	4.96	4.10	3.71	3.48	3.33	3.22	3.14	3.07	3.02	2.98
11	4.84	3.98	3.59	3.36	3.20	3.09	3.01	2.95	2.90	2.85
12	4.75	3.89	3.49	3.26	3.11	3.00	3.91	2.85	2.80	2.75
13	4.67	3.81	3.41	3.18	3.03	2.92	3.83	2.77	2.71	2.67
14	4.60	3.74	3.34	3.11	2.96	2.85	2.76	2.70	2.65	2.60
15	4.54	3.68	3.29	3.06	2.90	2.79	2.71	2.64	2.59	2.54
16	4.49	3.63	3.24	3.01	2.85	2.74	2.66	2.59	2.54	2.49
17	4.45	3.59	3.20	2.96	2.81	2.70	2.61	2.55	2.49	2.45
18	4.41	3.55	3.16	2.93	2.77	2.66	2.58	2.51	2.46	2.41
19	4.38	3.52	3.13	2.90	2.74	2.63	2.54	2.46	2.42	2.38
20	4.35	3.49	3.10	2.87	2.71	2.60	2.51	2.45	2.39	2.35
22	4.30	3.44	3.05	2.82	2.66	2.55	2.46	2.40	2.34	2.30
24	4.26	3.40	3.01	2.78	2.62	2.51	2.42	2.36	2.30	2.25
26	4.23	3.37	2.98	2.74	2.59	2.47	2.39	2.32	2.27	2.22
28	4.20	3.34	2.95	2.71	2.56	2.45	2.36	2.29	2.24	2.19
30	4.17	3.32	2.92	2.69	2.53	2.42	2.33	2.27	2.21	2.16
40	4.08	3.23	2.84	2.61	2.45	2.34	2.25	2.18	2.12	2.08
60	4.00	3.15	2.76	2.53	2.37	2.25	2.17	2.10	2.04	1.99
120	3.92	3.07	2.68	2.45	2.29	2.18	2.09	2.02	1.96	1.91
500	3.86	3.01	2.62	2.39	2.23	2.12	2.03	1.96	1.90	1.85
1000	3.85	3.01	2.61	2.38	2.22	2.11	2.02	1.95	1.89	1.84

APPENDIX C: (*Continued*)

df denom-inator	df Numerator									
	1	*2*	*3*	*4*	*5*	*6*	*7*	*8*	*9*	*10*
					$\alpha = .01$					
1	4048	4993	5377	5577	5668	5924	5992	6098	6132	6168
2	98.50	99.01	99.15	99.23	99.30	99.33	99.35	99.39	99.40	99.43
3	34.12	30.82	29.46	28.71	28.24	27.91	27.67	27.45	27.34	27.23
4	21.20	18.00	16.69	15.98	15.52	15.21	14.98	14.80	14.66	14.55
5	16.26	13.27	12.06	11.39	10.97	10.67	10.46	10.29	10.16	10.05
6	13.75	10.92	9.78	9.15	8.75	8.47	8.25	8.10	7.98	7.87
7	12.25	9.55	8.45	7.85	7.46	7.19	6.99	6.82	6.72	6.62
8	11.26	8.65	7.59	7.01	6.63	6.37	6.18	6.03	5.91	5.81
9	10.56	8.02	6.99	6.42	6.06	5.80	5.61	5.47	5.35	5.26
10	10.04	7.56	6.55	5.99	5.65	5.39	5.20	5.08	4.94	4.85
11	9.65	7.21	6.22	5.67	5.32	5.07	4.89	4.74	4.63	4.54
12	9.33	6.93	5.95	5.41	5.06	4.82	4.64	4.50	4.39	4.30
13	9.07	6.70	5.74	5.21	4.86	4.62	4.44	4.30	4.19	4.10
14	8.86	6.51	5.56	5.04	4.69	4.46	4.28	4.24	4.03	3.94
15	8.68	6.36	5.42	4.89	4.56	4.32	4.24	4.00	3.89	3.80
16	8.53	6.23	5.29	4.77	4.44	4.20	4.03	3.89	3.78	3.69
17	8.40	6.11	5.18	4.67	4.34	4.10	3.93	3.79	3.68	3.59
18	8.29	6.01	5.09	4.58	4.25	4.01	3.84	3.71	3.60	3.51
19	8.18	5.93	5.01	4.50	4.17	3.94	3.77	3.63	3.52	3.43
20	8.10	5.85	4.94	4.43	4.10	3.87	3.70	3.56	3.46	3.37
22	7.95	5.72	4.82	4.31	3.99	3.76	3.59	3.45	3.35	3.26
24	7.82	5.61	4.72	4.22	3.90	3.67	3.50	3.36	3.26	3.17
26	7.72	5.53	4.64	4.14	3.82	3.59	3.42	3.29	3.18	3.09
28	7.64	5.45	4.57	4.07	3.75	3.53	3.36	3.23	3.12	3.03
30	7.56	5.39	4.51	4.02	3.70	3.47	3.30	3.17	3.02	2.98
40	7.31	5.18	4.31	3.83	3.51	3.29	3.12	2.99	2.89	2.80
60	7.08	4.98	4.13	3.65	3.34	3.12	2.95	2.82	2.72	2.63
120	6.85	4.79	3.95	3.48	3.17	2.96	2.79	2.66	2.56	2.47
500	6.69	4.65	3.82	3.36	3.05	2.84	2.68	2.55	2.44	2.36
1000	6.67	4.63	3.80	3.34	3.04	2.82	2.66	2.53	2.43	2.34

Taken from D. C. Howell (1987), *Statistical Methods for Psychology*, 2nd ed., PWS Publishing Co., Boston, MA, by permission of the publisher.

APPENDIX D: DISTRIBUTION OF χ^2

n	.30	.20	.10	.05	.02	.01	.001
1	1.07	1.64	2.71	3.84	5.41	6.64	10.83
2	2.41	3.22	4.60	5.99	7.82	9.21	13.82
3	3.66	4.64	6.25	7.82	9.84	11.34	16.27
4	4.88	5.89	7.78	9.49	11.67	13.28	18.46
5	6.06	7.29	9.24	11.07	13.39	15.09	20.52
6	7.23	8.56	10.64	12.59	15.03	16.81	22.46
7	8.38	9.80	12.02	14.07	16.62	18.48	24.32
8	9.52	11.03	13.34	15.51	18.17	20.09	26.12
9	10.06	12.24	14.68	16.92	19.68	21.67	27.88
10	11.78	13.44	15.88	18.31	21.16	23.21	29.59
11	12.80	14.83	17.28	19.68	22.62	24.72	31.26
12	14.01	15.81	18.55	21.03	24.05	23.22	32.91
13	15.12	16.98	19.81	22.36	25.47	27.69	34.53
14	16.22	18.15	21.09	23.68	26.87	29.14	36.12
15	17.32	19.31	22.31	25.00	28.26	30.58	37.70
16	18.42	20.46	23.54	26.30	29.63	32.00	39.25
17	19.51	21.62	24.77	27.59	31.00	33.41	40.79
18	20.60	22.70	25.99	28.87	32.35	34.80	42.31
19	21.69	23.90	27.20	30.14	33.69	36.19	43.82
20	22.78	25.04	28.41	31.41	35.02	37.57	45.32
21	23.86	26.17	29.62	32.67	36.34	38.93	46.80
22	24.94	27.30	30.81	33.92	37.66	40.29	48.27
23	26.02	28.43	32.01	35.17	38.97	41.64	49.73
24	27.10	29.55	33.20	36.42	40.27	42.98	51.18
25	28.17	30.68	34.38	37.65	41.57	44.31	52.62
26	29.25	31.80	35.56	38.88	42.86	45.64	54.05
27	30.32	32.91	36.74	40.11	44.14	46.96	55.48
28	31.39	34.03	37.92	41.34	45.42	48.28	56.89
29	32.46	35.14	39.09	42.56	46.69	49.59	58.30
30	33.53	36.25	40.26	43.77	47.96	50.89	59.70

Abridged from Table III of Fisher (1942), *Statistical Methods for Research Workers*, 3rd ed., Oliver and Boyd, Ltd., Edinburgh, by permission of the publishers.

GLOSSARY OF TERMS

Alternative hypothesis: Hypothesis that states that there are differences between experimental conditions. This hypothesis is supported indirectly when the null hypothesis is rejected.

Before-and-after design: Research design in which the same subjects' performance is compared before and after some event or experimental intervention.

Between-groups design: Experimental design in which different subjects are assigned to different experimental conditions.

Between-groups variance: A measure of how group means differ from each other; used as the numerator term in the F test for analysis of variance.

Carryover effects: The impact on later behavior of earlier events and reactions to them.

Causal relationship: Relationship between two variables in which changes in one variable can be identified as leading to changes in the other variable. The experimental method is particularly well suited for determining such cause-and-effect relationships.

Causality: Assessment of which variables are responsible for observed changes in a particular behavior.

Chance sampling effects: Differences in the distribution of subject characteristics between different random samples from the same population.

Confidence interval: Range of values of a statistic such as the mean within which the population value will fall for a fixed percentage of randomly selected samples. This range is useful for pinning down plausible values of a population value based on observations from a sample.

Confounding: When changes in behavior are due to the influence of two or more variables whose effects cannot be separated. Various control procedures are designed to eliminate or reduce confounding influences of extraneous variables. Factorial designs permit the separate analysis of more than one variable in the same study.

Control: Equating or holding constant the effects of some variable so that that variable will not influence the results of a research study.

Counterbalancing: Procedure used in a within-subject design by which subjects are assigned to different sequences of experimental conditions such that the effects of progressive changes in behavior (e.g., practice effects) are equated across experimental conditions.

Critical region: Extreme values of the distribution of a statistical test leading to rejection of the null hypothesis. The probability that sample data will lead to such values if the null hypothesis is true is α.

Critical value: Tabled values for distributions such as t, F, and χ^2, which determine the boundary of the critical region. Obtaining a statistical value more extreme than this leads to rejection of the null hypothesis.

Degrees of freedom: Value used to determine the *critical region* for a particular statistical test; corresponds to the number of independent observations in a set of scores about which a hypothesis has been formulated.

Dependent variable: Behavior or response recorded by the experimenter.

Descriptive statistics: Statistical summaries of data obtained from a sample of observations.

Effect size: A standardized measure of the magnitude of an experimental effect, such as the difference between the mean scores for experimental and control conditions divided by the standard deviation for the control condition; often used in meta-analyses that attempt to compare results across studies.

Experimental method: Research method characterized by the manipulation of one or more variables (independent variables) and the control of all others.

Experimenter bias: How the experimenter's expectations about the results of an experiment may affect the measurement and interpretation of data.

Extraneous variable: A variable other than the manipulated independent variable that could influence the results of an experiment. Control of such variables is a key feature of the experimental method.

Factorial design: Research design in which more than one independent variable is manipulated and all combinations of the selected levels of the independent variables are included.

Fractional factorial design: Research design with several independent variables in which not all combinations are included; systematically select those combinations that provide the most information about the effects of the variables.

Hypothesis testing: Using data from samples to test whether populations are the same or different.

Independent random groups design: Experimental design in which different subjects are assigned at random to different experimental conditions.

Independent variable: Variable manipulated by the experimenter using the experimental method.

Inferential statistics: The process of inference by which characteristics of populations are learned by analyzing the characteristics of samples taken from the population.

Interaction: Statistical measure of the extent to which the effect of one variable differs at different levels of another variable; determined through analysis of variance of a factorial design.

Interval scale: Scale of measurement that indicates the magnitude of difference or distance between values. These scales have the property of equal intervals between consecutive values on the scale, but have an arbitrary zero point. Examples are test scores and attitude scales. Hypotheses concerning these data can be tested with t or F.

Level of significance: Choice of acceptable Type I error rate (α) based on consideration of relative consequences of making a Type I or a Type II error.

Linear relation: Relationship between two variables that, when plotted on a graph, is best fit by a straight line.

Longitudinal study: Study in which the same sample of individuals is followed over a long period of time.

Main effects: In a study involving multiple variables, the effect of each variable averaged over levels of the other variables; term used in analysis of variance.

Manipulation: Using the experimental method and creating or identifying discrete levels of the independent variable. Subjects are randomly assigned to the different levels.

Matched pairs: Assigning subjects to experimental conditions by taking two subjects with similar values on some subject variable and randomly assigning one of them to one condition and the other to the other condition.

Matching: Assigning subjects to conditions in a between-subjects design by equating the conditions on selected subject variables.

Mean: Measure of the average of a set of scores, sometimes called the arithmetic average, calculated by summing all the scores and dividing by the number of scores.

Median: Measure of the average of a set of scores obtained by rank ordering all the scores and finding the value that divides the set in half, with half the scores above that value and half below it.

Meta-analysis: A quantitative method for combining the results of many different studies of the same phenomenon. Used to assess the reliability of an experimental effect and to determine factors that moderate the size of the effect.

Method of indirect proof: Strategy used in hypothesis testing by which the alternative hypothesis is supported when the null hypothesis is discredited.

Method of observation: Research method characterized by recording of naturally occurring events and relationships, without intervention on the part of the researcher.

Mode: Measure of the average of a set of scores representing the score value that occurs more frequently than other values in its vicinity. There may be more than one mode (e.g., a bimodal distribution has two modes).

Multifactor ANOVA: Analysis of variance used in conjunction with research employing a factorial design; includes F tests of hypotheses about each separate variable (main effects) and the interactions between variables.

Multiple regression equation: Equation that predicts the value of a criterion variable (Y) on the basis of a weighted sum of the values of a set of predictor variables (Xs).

Nominal scale: Scale of measurement used only to designate different categories such as political party affiliation or which brand was selected by a consumer. Hypotheses concerning these data are usually tested with χ^2.

Nonparametric tests: Statistical tests of significance that do not rely on assumptions about the forms of sampling distributions; sometimes called *distribution-free tests*.

Normal distribution: A continuous distribution of scores specified by a mathematical equation typically translated into a table of probabilities that specify the area beneath the curve cut off by intervals such as the area between the mean and varying standard deviation units above the mean. The normal distribution or "normal curve" is symmetrical or "bell shaped," meaning that the mean, median, and mode are all equal and that scores further from the mean occur less frequently.

Null hypothesis: Hypothesis initially assumed true. Usually the hypothesis of no effect of the variable of interest or the hypothesis that the researcher hopes to "nullify."

One-tailed test: Statistical test in which the critical region is concentrated at one end of the distribution of the statistic; used when the researcher has a unidirectional prediction of the results.

One-way ANOVA: Analysis of variance used in conjunction with research focusing on the influence of a single variable with several levels.

Order relations: Comparisons of data based only on whether one value is higher than (e.g., preferred to) another value, not on the basis of how much difference there is between them.

Ordinal scale: Scale of measurement that indicates the relative order of magnitude of different responses, but does not give any information about differences between responses. Hypotheses concerning these data are tested with nonparametric methods such as the Mann–Whitney U test.

Population: The complete set of all possible observations for a research study. In practice, only a sample of observations from the population is used.

Power: The probability of correctly rejecting the null hypothesis when it is false. Mathematically, power is equal to 1 minus the probability of Type II error, or $P = 1 - \beta$.

Proportion of variance accounted for: A measure of the strength of association between independent (X) and dependent (Y) variables or the predictive power afforded by a relationship. When this value is zero, then X does not aid us at all in predicting the value of Y; when it is 1.00, then X tells us exactly what Y is. Intermediate values represent different degrees of predictive ability.

p **Value:**   The probability of obtaining the observed value or a more extreme value for a test statistic if the null hypothesis is true. Used as an index of the likelihood that the null hypothesis is true.

Quasi-experimental design: Research design that attempts to approximate a true experiment by controlling as many variables as possible, but without the ability to assign subjects at random to different conditions.

Random assignment: Assigning subjects to experimental conditions such that each subject has the same chance as any other subject of being placed in any condition; usually involves consulting a table of random numbers.

Random sampling: Selecting subjects from a population such that each member of the population has an equal chance of being selected.

Randomization: Method of assigning subjects to experimental conditions such that each subject has an equal chance of being selected for any condition; same as *random assignment.*

Randomized blocks design: Experimental design in which subjects are grouped into blocks such that the blocks will be more alike in their responses, apart from any experimental effect, than will be subjects selected completely at random; a form of matching used to control for subject variables.

Ratio scale: Scale of measurement that provides the best match to the real number system by possessing a constant unit and a true zero point, thus permitting designation of difference, sum, product, and ratio of values. Examples are number of errors on a task and time to complete a response. Hypotheses concerning these data can be tested with *t* or *F*.

Regression line: Line that best fits a *scatter diagram* such that the squared differences between the *Y* values of the actual points and the values on the line are less than for any other line; also known as *prediction line* or *line of best fit.*

Repeated measures design: Research design in which measures of behavior are obtained from the same individuals under different conditions; also known as *within-subject design.*

Sample: The subset of observations from a larger population actually selected for use in a research study.

Sample statistics: The value of a statistical measure such as mean, median, mode, or standard deviation, calculated for a sample of scores.

Sampling distribution: Distribution of values of a statistic such as the mean for different random samples of the same size from the same population.

Sampling error: The extent to which sample statistics will vary from sample to sample even when the samples are selected at random from the same population.

Scatter diagram: A plot of the relationship between two variables X and Y showing the pattern of X-Y points in two-dimensional space.

Standard deviation: Measure of variability of a set of scores obtained by taking the square root of the sum of squared differences between each score and the mean of the scores, divided by the number of scores (or the number minus 1 when using a sample standard deviation to estimate the population standard deviation).

Standard error: The standard deviation of a sampling distribution; used in computing confidence intervals as well as in hypothesis testing.

Standard score transformation: The score value minus the mean of the score, then divided by the standard deviation. This value represents the location of the score in terms of number of standard deviation units above or below the mean, and is not dependent on units of measurement.

Statistically significant result: Results of a statistical test leading to rejection of the null hypothesis.

Subject biases: How subjects' beliefs about how they should act in a particular research setting affect their behavior.

Subject variables: Subject characteristics that distinguish one subject from another in an experiment and can affect the results of the experiment.

Test of contingency: χ^2 applied to studies in which a subject is classified in terms of two different variables; sometimes known as *tests of independence*, analogous to interaction tests in ANOVA.

Time-lag method: Studying changes in attitude and behavior across a relatively long period of time; also known as *longitudinal study*.

Two-tailed test: Statistical test in which the critical region is divided between both ends of the distribution of the statistic; used when there is no a priori prediction of a directional effect.

Two-way ANOVA: Analysis of variance applied to a factorial design involving two variables.

Type I error: Rejecting a true null hypothesis; its probability is called α.

Type II error: Retaining a false null hypothesis; its probability is called β.

Unbiased estimate: Sample statistics such as the mean whose distribution is centered around the true population value; for example, the mean of a set of random sample means equals the mean of the population from which the samples were drawn.

Variance: The square of standard deviation. Thus, whereas the standard deviation is expressed in a unit of measurement (e.g., inches), the variance is expressed in squared units (e.g., squared inches).

Within-group variance: A measure of how individuals within the same group differ from each other; used as the denominator or measure of *chance sampling effects* in the F test for analysis of variance.

Within-subject design: Experimental design in which each subject receives every level of the independent variable; also known as *repeated measures* design.

Within-subject manipulation: A variable whose effects are determined by examining how the same subjects' responses differ across different levels of the variable.

NOTES

1. Our discussion of causality will focus on the role of research methodology in establishing cause-and-effect. Readers might also be interested in the broader philosophical/scientific discussion of causality provided by Hempel's (1965) essay, "Aspects of scientific explanation."

2. Even surveys and questionnaires which do not attempt to manipulate behavior or assign respondents to different experimental conditions are often administered in controlled settings such as testing rooms. This is done to assure high completion rates, to allow for uniform instructions and answering of participants' questions, to minimize distractions, and to observe behavior under relatively constant conditions.

3. The effect of departures from the assumptions of normality and equal variances will be to make the probabilities associated with the t test to be not exactly equal to those that are tabled. However, the exact probability of a difference between two means is pertinent only if the test of significance gives a borderline result.

4. When the degrees of freedom are sufficiently large (> 30) or when population standard deviations are known and do not have to be estimated from sample data, a table of the normal curve or z test can be used to obtain "critical values." However, because the t test is more general, we include it here and omit the z test.

5. It is almost certain that calculations as complicated as these would be done on the computer. We present the computational procedures here to show where the numbers on the computer printout come from, what they mean, and the logic behind their derivation.

REFERENCES

BROWN, S. R., and MELAMED, L. E. (1990). *Experimental design and analysis* (Sage University Papers Series on Quantitative Applications in the Social Sciences, series no. 07-74). Thousand Oaks, CA: Sage.

DOMINOWSKI, R. L. (1980). *Research methods.* Englewood Cliffs, NJ: Prentice-Hall.

EDWARDS, A. L. (1968). *Experimental design in psychological research*, 3rd ed. New York: Holt, Rinehart & Winston.

GARDNER, P. L. (1975). Scales and statistics. *Review of Educational Research, 45,* 43–57.

HARRIS, M. B. (1998). *Basic statistics for behavioral science research,* 2nd ed. Boston, MA: Allyn and Bacon.

HAYS, W. L. (1994). *Statistics,* 5th ed. Fort Worth, TX: Harcourt Brace.

HEDGES, L. V., SHYMANSKY, J., and WOODWORTH, B. (1989). *A practical guide to modern methods of meta analysis.* Washington, DC: National Science Teachers Association.

HEMPEL, C. (1965). *Aspects of scientific explanation and other essays.* New York: The Free Press.

HENKEL, R. E. (1976). *Tests of significance* (Sage University Papers Series on Quantitative Applications in the Social Sciences, series no. 07-4). Thousand Oaks, CA: Sage.

HOPKINS, K. D., HOPKINS, B. R., and GLASS, G. V. (1996). *Basic statistics for the behavioral sciences,* 3rd ed. Boston, MA: Allyn and Bacon.

IVERSEN, G. R., and NORPOTH, H. (1976). *Analysis of variance,* 2nd ed. (Sage University Papers Series on Quantitative Applications in the Social Sciences, series no. 07-1). Thousand Oaks, CA: Sage.

JACKSON, S., and BRASHERS, D. E. (1994). *Random factors in ANOVA* (Sage University Papers Series on Quantitative Applications in the Social Sciences, series no. 07-98). Thousand Oaks, CA: Sage.

JOHN, O. P., DONAHUE, E. M., and KENTLE, R. L. (1991). *The big five inventory,* Versions 4a and 54. Technical Report, University of California, Institute of Personality and Social Research.

KANTOWITZ, B. H., ROEDIGER, H. L., III, and ELMES, D. G. (1994). *Experimental psychology: Understanding psychological research,* 5th ed. Minneapolis-St. Paul, MN: West.

KIRK, R. E. (1982). *Experimental design: Procedures for the behavioral sciences,* 2nd ed. Belmont, CA: Brooks/Cole.

LEFKOWITZ, M. M., ERON, L. D., WALDER, L. O., and HUESMANN, L. R. (1977). *Growing up to be violent.* New York: Pergamon.

LEVIN, I. P., and HINRICHS, J. V. (1995). *Experimental psychology: Contemporary methods and applications.* Madison, WI: Brown & Benchmark.

LEWIS-BECK, M. S. (1980). *Applied regression* (Sage University Papers Series on Quantitative Applications in the Social Sciences, series no. 07-22). Thousand Oaks, CA: Sage.

LIEBETRAU, A. M. (1983). *Measures of association* (Sage University Papers Series on Quantitative Applications in the Social Sciences, series no. 07-32). Thousand Oaks, CA: Sage.

LOUVIERE, J. J. (1988). *Analyzing decision making: Metric conjoint analysis* (Sage University Papers Series on Quantitative Applications in the Social Sciences, series no. 07-67). Thousand Oaks, CA: Sage.

MCNEMAR, Q. (1969). *Psychological Statistics*, 4th ed. New York: Wiley.

MOHR, L. B. (1990). *Understanding significance testing* (Sage University Papers Series on Quantitative Applications in the Social Sciences, series no. 07-73). Thousand Oaks, CA: Sage.

SCHROEDER, L. D., SJOQUIST, D. L., and STEPHAN, P. E. (1986). *Understanding regression analysis* (Sage University Papers Series on Quantitative Applications in the Social Sciences, series no. 07-57). Thousand Oaks, CA: Sage.

SHAUGHNESSY, J. J., and ZECHMEISTER, E. B. (1985). *Research methods in psychology*. New York: Knopf.

SIEGEL, S. (1956). *Nonparametric statistics for the behavioural sciences*. New York: McGraw-Hill.

SIEGEL, S., and CASTELLAN, N. J., JR. (1988). *Nonparametric statistics for the behavioral sciences*, 2nd ed. New York: McGraw-Hill.

SMITH, M. S., and GLASS, A. L. (1977). Meta-analysis of psychotherapy outcome studies. *American Psychologist, 32,* 752–760.

WINER, B. J., BROWN, D. R., and MICHELS, K. M. (1991). *Statistical principles in experimental design*, 3rd ed. New York: McGraw-Hill.

ABOUT THE AUTHOR

IRWIN P. LEVIN is a Professor in the Department of Psychology, with a joint appointment in the Department of Marketing, at the University of Iowa. He received his PhD from the University of California at Los Angeles. He teaches courses in behavioral research methodology and conducts research in the pyschology of judgment and decision making. He is currently President of the Society for Judgment and Decision Making.